SURVIVAL GUIDE FOR OUTSIDERS

or

How to protect yourself from

Politicians, Experts, & Other Insiders

by

Sherman K. Stein

Survival Guide for Outsiders:
How to Protect Yourself from Politicians, Experts, & Other Insiders
Author: Sherman K. Stein
Copyright Sherman K. Stein, 2010
Cataloging information
Library of Congress Control Number: 2009908100
ISBN-1-4392-5327-7

Other books by Sherman K. Stein:

Mathematics: The Man-Made Universe

Calculus and Analytic Geometry

Algebra and Tiling

Strength in Numbers

Archimedes: What Did He Do Besides Cry Eureka?

How the Other Half Thinks.

Published in the United States of America
See Colophon at the end of the book for further information.

SURVIVAL GUIDE FOR OUTSIDERS

"In this moment of crisis we all ought to support the President. He is the man who has all the information and knowledge of what we are up against."

— Governor Nelson Rockefeller, commenting on mass demonstrations against the Vietnam War in *The New York Times*, February 1, 1966

"Some ... may believe that there exists a body of secret information which gives officials in the Executive branch of our government special insight which enables them better to determine courses of action which will serve the national interest. This is questionable. ...

...Our growing involvement in Vietnam and the question of whether that involvement serves the interests of the United States is hardly a case to be decided upon the basis of information not available to the conscientious citizen. On national issues of this kind decisions turn not upon available facts but upon judgment. There is no secret information or magical formula which gives Presidential advisors wisdom and judgment on broad policy but which is not available to the intelligent citizen."

— Senator J. William Fulbright, in his Introduction to *The Vietnam Hearings*, Random House, 1966

Contents

Preamble: Why I Wrote This Book

Back at the height of the cold war, I lived in a little town in the Central Valley of California. I wasn't worried about nuclear bombs because my town would surely not be a target. It was, however, surrounded by a triangle of Air Force bases: Sacramento to the east, Marysville to the North, and Fairfield to the southwest. These were all prime targets in the case of what is euphemistically called a "nuclear exchange," for lack of a better phrase. The blast probably wouldn't reach me, but the radioactive debris would, carried by the winds.

So naked self-interest turned me into a nuclear activist. I read everything I could about the missiles, their accuracy and throw weight, the size of the payload, the effects of atomic and hydrogen bombs, the radius of total destruction, the radius of lethal radiation, and the long-term impact. It became obvious that the only use for these bombs was to discourage other nations from using them. I refuse to call them "weapons," for the destruction they inflict is disproportionate to any possible political gain.

The naval historian Bernard Brodie reached the same conclusion long before in a twenty-eight-page memorandum, *The Atomic Bomb and American Security*, dated November 1, 1945, less than three months after we dropped the bombs on Japan. His analysis remains as valid today as it was over sixty years ago.

Among the books I read were Henry Kissinger's *Nuclear Weapons and Foreign Policy* and Herman Kahn's *On Thermonuclear War*. Kissinger argued that there could be a limited nuclear war, which the contestants would not allow to ratchet out of control. Kahn claimed that after a nuclear war, in which we might suffer a hundred million dead, we would eventually bounce back to normal life, though it might take a century. Both books struck me as nonsense.

But who was I, earning my living as a mathematician, far from the centers where the big decisions were being made, to dare have an opinion about what those experts asserted? They spent all their waking hours gathering information, talking to fellow experts, and drawing conclusions. I had little time after lecturing, making and grading exams, serving on university and department committees, to devote to contemplating the niceties of nuclear bombs.

On the other hand, who were they to write books on nuclear war? After all, there had never been such a war. Our dropping two atomic bombs in 1945 – all we had at the time – on a nation that had none certainly offered no useful precedent. What did Kissinger and Kahn know that I didn't? What, in short, made them experts and me just a layperson who should bow down to their superior wisdom? Did they, like doctors, have a certificate on the wall from some institution, showing that they were especially qualified to pontificate on nuclear war, which could include the exchange of thousands of warheads, each far more destructive than the bombs that burst over Hiroshima and Nagasaki?

From asking those questions it was but a small step to raise more general questions: What makes an expert an expert? How do I recognize that a person is an expert? If the alleged expert cannot produce a certificate with Gothic letters and a gold seal, what are the criteria I should look for? How do some people achieve the designation as being wiser than the rest of us, so that their predictions and proposals are treated with singular respect?

I thought about what experts do and observed their role in our society. That led me to think about how anyone chooses between one course of action and another. Everywhere I looked I saw limits on how smart anyone, expert or layperson, can be in making choices. Eventually I put my thoughts together in this book.

Real-world examples illustrate my thinking. You can easily provide illustrations from your own experience. I lay my evidence on the table, exposed like the steps in a mathematical argument. You don't have to accept anything

I say on faith. In fact, and this is a theme running through the chapters, you don't have to accept on faith what anyone says.

I think of this book as a manual for us laypersons trying to participate in a healthy democracy, whose survival, as Jefferson wrote, depends on an informed citizenry:

> *"Whenever the people are well-informed, they can be trusted with their own government ... whenever things go so far wrong as to attract their notice, they may be relied on to set them to rights."*

What I Will Do

In Chapter 1 I set the stage for everything that follows. It points out that we effortlessly build an image of the world within our skulls. I call this image "the model." That world, not the one "out there," becomes the basis for our choices and actions. Yet it is fragile, easily manipulated by those in a position to influence us. All this will surprise no one, but I want it on the record, for emphasis. The next two chapters show why we are so vulnerable.

In Chapters 4 through 7, I describe two ways by which people operate on our minds, and how to guard ourselves from them. There may be few surprises in these opening chapters. Even so, they remind us in detail why we can be easily played for fools.

Chapters 8 and 9 distinguish two types of choices that we make, and why they limit our ability to control what will unfold in the future. We might hope that we could make our choices more logically, even with the aid of numbers, but Chapters 10 to 17 show why this route to greater wisdom also has limits. That is the only part of the book where I use what I learned in my daytime job as a mathematician, but I use it to show that mathematics will not get us out of our difficulties.

Chapter 18 concerns jobs and their two separate roles: to divide up the work to be done and to distribute the rewards for doing that work. Both roles are crucial to making decisions and for building a functionng society.

All told, the first eighteen chapters show why we can be only so wise in our efforts to control the future. The remaining chapters describe how we try to act more wisely, as individuals and as a society. It is at this point that I face the issues of expertise raised by Kissinger and Kahn.

Most of the remaining chapters are about experts. What are they? How do we identify them? How can we protect ourselves from them?

Psychologists, sociologists, futurologists, economists, anthropologists, and political scientists have studied many of the topics that I touch on. I've drawn on some of their work, but for the most part base my case on my own experience. If I fail to mention pertinent research that would reinforce or contradict what I write, I apologize. This is not a scholarly work. My goal is to provide a manual for living in a democracy. I try to develop an attitude, and from that attitude certain techniques emerge.

I could not omit any of the ideas. As you look back over the chapters, you will see that they fit together like pieces in a jigsaw puzzle.

ACKNOWLEDGMENTS

All my other books have been about mathematics, so I needed help when I ventured to write about the wide world where choices are made, decisions reached, and actions with unforeseen consequences are undertaken. The little bit of mathematics in this book has only one purpose: to show that mathematics will not rescue us from the inevitable imperfections of the way we think and act. At best, mathematics will only provide an illusion of "rationality," a word I have not been able to define.

During the many years that I worked on this book, off and on, I was encouraged to persist by a variety of signals:

The *Sacramento Bee* published two of my Op-Ed articles; one developed into Chapters 19 to 22, on Experts, and the other into Chapter 17, *The GRIMP*, which deals with the way we cope with gigantic enterprises that may fail.

Years after they had seen an early version, two readers, independently sent me long e-mails describing how the book changed the way they had viewed the world.

A woman who had never met me before told me that she read the whole Chapter 29, *The Action Syndrome*, to a friend over the phone. She asked me where I got it. I explained that I got it from just watching how people, including myself, act.

Regrettably, I no longer have their names. Perhaps they will come upon this book and help me acknowledge their role.

But I do have the names of several others who have helped shape the book: Peter Renz, mathematician and editor; my wife, the poet Hannah Stein, and Peter Westfall, statistician and former editor of *The American Statistician*, made many suggestions that clarified the entire manuscript. Various chapters were improved by Barbara Archer, publicist.

I am indebted to a number of specialists who read the manuscript and made suggestions, among them: Maya Bar-Hillel of the Center for Rationality at Hebrew University; Don Chakerian, mathematician and philosopher; Paul Goldstene, political scientist; Steven Piker, anthropologist and sociologist, Robin Hogarth, former head of the Center for Decision Research at the University of Chicago; John Paulos, author of *Innumeracy,* Judy Snyder, retired magnet school teacher; Larry Snyder, musician and musicologist, Philip Tetlock, author of *Expert Political Judgment: How good Is It?;* Ken Watt, ecologist, and Mary Wind, president of TeachPeace.

The cartoons are by John Johnson and the diagrams by Peter Renz. My thanks to both for their contributions to the the book.

PERCEPTION

1 The Model and Us Frivolous Ones

A simple experiment: Some options.

At this moment insiders are plotting how to control our brains. As former White House press secretary Scott McClellan put it, their tools are "spin, stonewalling, hedging, evasion, denial, noncommunication, and deceit by omission." This book offers techniques for defending ourselves from such machinations.

If the real world were as tidy as mathematics, I wouldn't have to write this book. In my daytime job, two plus three is always five, everyone agrees on the basic assumptions, and we draw conclusions with a chain of reasons that obey rules as strict as those that govern a game of baseball.

But outside this ivory tower, the world is a madhouse. Practicing mathematics has made me hypersensitive to the way decisions are made in the real world, where there are no accepted basic assumptions as starting points, and no restrictions on how to draw conclusions from them. It is a Wild West of the mind.

In the world of mathematics we speak to the intellect. Each step is explicit and can be checked. Not so in human affairs, where rhetoric is aimed at the gut, and it is usually impossible to check whether it is right or wrong.

Gut reasoning, imprecision, and lack of checkable facts would be of little importance if we lived under a dictator. But we live in a democracy, and, like it or not, we are the ultimate check in a delicate system of checks and balances.

There are many of us, but we are a frivolous bunch. We are no match for those who make a fulltime career of governing or running a corporation day in and day out. We must make our modest contributions in our spare time. No wonder we are vulnerable.

I say vulnerable because we are easily convinced by the flimsiest evidence. This tendency was critical to our survival when the challenges we faced required quick decisions: flee or fight. In our present world, where the challenges are complex, such a response is our undoing. Review the disasters of the twentieth century and you will see that our wisdom has not kept up with the new options that magnify our powers to do good or to inflict harm. Technical progress has made parts of your brain and mine obsolete. We all, both high and low, ought to be far more humble than we are.

For every issue of the day, whether local or national, we form an opinion, a belief, an attitude, a perception, call it what you will. When a pollster phones us, we feel important and are happy to reveal where we stand even though we may not have spent more than a few minutes studying the issue.

To illustrate this tendency, let's start with a simple optical illusion. I pick it because it's not one of the controversies that keep us on a high emotional red alert.

I had thought of using an example that we already share, such as our attitudes during the buildup to the Iraq invasion. Take mine, for instance. At first I felt it was a dumb idea, because wars in general have horrible, unpredictable consequences, even for the victor.

Then I was reminded that Saddam committed terrible crimes, so thought the invasion was a good idea. Next, hearing that the international inspectors had found no sign of weapons of mass destruction, I changed my mind again.

But then the big shots at the top of government warned me that Saddam could unleash a mushroom cloud in a mere forty-five

minutes. Who was I to condemn a whole city to mass extermina-
tion? Surely the big shots knew something that I did not for they
have access to at least forty billion dollars worth of intelligence
per year, (that's over a hundred million dollars a day) collected by
the CIA, the National Security Agency, Defense Intelligence Agency,
National Reconnaissance Agency, National Geospatial-Intelligence
Agency, Homeland Office of Intelligence Analysis, State Department Bureau of Intelligence and Research, Army Intelligence and
Security Command, Office of Naval Intelligence, Air Force Intelligence Agency, and on and on. And the president even had the
service of the President's Foreign Intelligence Advisory Board to
help him analyze the analysis. Who was I to suspect that they
were feeding me hokum?

On the basis of that scary image of a mushroom cloud rising
high into the sky, I probably would have voted to invade, though
that vote, within my mind, was close, like 51 to 49. Because I had
never been to Iraq, knew not a single Iraqi, never studied the history of Iraq, I was easily pulled one way and then the other while
going about my daily chores on my bicycle in the flat little town
of Davis, California.

My point is not whether it was wise or foolish to invade. Rather
it is that I could look at the information leading up the invasion
in many different ways, but at any moment I simply had to have
a viewpoint, a perspective, as though I were sitting in the Senate
and was obliged to vote.

Instead of Iraq, I will now use a cool, fresh, non-controversial
example, just a picture. I know it's much simpler than the events
about which we are constantly forming opinions. Even so, it illustrates a critical idea, which I will refer to often throughout the
coming chapters.

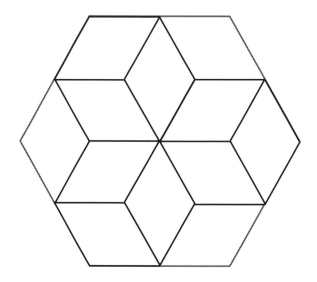

A SIMPLE EXPERIMENT

What do you see? Three cubes, with the top cube to the left? Three cubes, with the top cube to the right? A six-pointed star in a hexagon? Or is it just thirty identical line segments? Or do you see it as twelve parallelograms filling up a hexagon?

It seems impossible to stare at the picture and not give it some form. Inevitably, we interpret it. We cannot resist giving it meaning. That's how we deal with events in the real world. We don't just notice them. We fit them into our view of life. The process is so automatic that we are not aware of it. Even if we are aware we do it, it is hard to stop ourselves and, so to speak, stay on the sidelines.

Scientists call this habit of forming a perception "modeling." Physicists model the world. For instance, they say that any two objects attract each other with a force that shrinks the further apart they are. Modeling the universe with a few such assumptions, physicists deduce that planets move in elliptical orbits. They work within their models, not with the world itself. So do we. A model replaces a complex reality with something easier to deal with. It may be wrong. It may oversimplify. But at least it's in our heads and we can work with it.

Here is an example from my own experience to show how we do this.

While taking a walk I noticed a school bus parked on the street opposite an elementary school. On its side was the name of a school district in a nearby town. "Oh," I said to myself, "it brought pupils on a visit here. Or maybe it's a local bus bought used and the old district's name hasn't been painted over." I couldn't just look at the bus as simply a big, yellow object with wheels. I felt compelled to give it a meaning. Both of my guesses were wrong. The driver explained that he had dropped high school students off at the university and then had driven about until he could find a parking place. My compulsion to model led me to the wrong conclusion, but this was of no consequence. My next example, however, has substantial implications.

SOME OPTIONS

Theology might be described as the making of a model for the whole universe, as the following actual incident illustrates. A certain mathematics department consisted mainly of devout professors, but there was an atheist in their midst, which upset them. A Jesuit priest was dispatched to cure him of his atheism. After much fruitless argument, the priest gave up and asked the atheist, "How do you know that there is no God?" The atheist replied, "There are some things you must take on faith."

That ended the discussion. Both priest and atheist had created their own models of the universe, both beyond proof or disproof. Each looked at the ultimate equivocal illusion, the universe itself, and saw radically different patterns. The Jesuit saw a guiding hand; the atheist did not. There was no halfway point of compromise

What is the basis of the conflict between the West and the Islamic world? A president of the United States said it is because they hate our freedoms. Osama bin Laden said that is not the reason; rather, it is because of United States policy and actions in the Middle East: "If it were from hatred of your freedoms we would have attacked Sweden." Both models cannot be right.

Deciding how to model our relation to the Muslim world is far more important than interpreting the optical illusion or the parked bus. But each of us has a model, and those models shape how we think about the conflicts in Iraq and Afghanistan, how we vote, and, ultimately, how our nation acts in the world. No matter how firmly held, our personal models of what is driving events in the Middle East are not generally grounded on direct knowledge of place, people, or events. Most of us haven't lived in the Middle East and we don't speak Arabic or Farsi. We probably know little of the history of the region. We have no idea when those straight-line borders separating the countries were established or who drew them. Our models are necessarily based on second- and third-hand accounts, amounting to little more than hearsay. I wonder how many of us could identify Afghanistan, Iraq, and Iran on a map that shows only borders, or just tell their order from west to east. How many could identify Mohammed Mossadegh?

That the bedrock of international affairs is not reality, but a model, is also illustrated by an example from a century ago. In this case we know which model turned out to be correct. That is one advantage of looking back, in contrast to paying attention only to the present.

Consider the two views of the pre-World War I armaments race, dominated by the construction of ever larger battleships by Germany and Great Britain. Pacifists, about to assemble for the Hague Peace Conference of 1907, saw that race as a threat to security. But Theodore Roosevelt, then president, saw the same race in an opposing light. In a letter of September, 1906, he wrote, "In the Hague, my chief trouble will come from the fantastic visionaries who are crazy to do the impossible. Just at present the United States Navy is an infinitely more potent factor for peace than all the peace societies."

Each year that passed with armaments increasing and without war breaking out confirmed his perception and weakened the pacifists' case. But the outbreak of World War I less than eight years after he wrote that letter can be seen as validating the fears of the 'fantastic visionaries.'

Real life can even be shaped by a perception of a perception of a perception, "perception raised to the third power." As President Johnson wrote about the Vietnam War in his memoirs: "I thought that Hanoi would probably view a new cessation in bombing as a sign of weakness." That short sentence describes three efforts to model, for it is a perception about a view about an attitude. He was modeling how Hanoi would model his modeling of the halt in bombing. Reality was buried under layers of hypotheses.

The world that shapes our actions is not the one "out there," but is the one that gradually forms inside our own skulls. I am fascinated by the unpredictably diverse ways different people, facing the same fact, can interpret it in opposite ways. If optical illusions thrive on the peculiarities of retina and optic nerve, how many errors of judgment spring from imperfections of that far more complex instrument, the brain.

The hand is quicker than the eye, and the world subtler than the mind. No wonder the chains of cause and effect in human affairs can be interpreted so many ways

At a magic show, where we know we are being misled, we are on guard. But outside the theater, in the wide world, no one warns us about the "magicians" who are trying to shape our models of the world. When we stop to think how weak are the foundations that support most of our views, we will realize how vulnerable we are and why it's so easy to play us for "suckers."

In the following chapters I will analyze why we are such push-overs, the techniques insiders use to manipulate us, and how we can protect ourselves.

2 The Bull's Eye and the Rings

The bull's eye; Perception and model;
Our hunger for the truth.

The foundation of a mathematical theory, such as geometry, is spelled out for all to see. It consists of a few clear-cut assumptions called "axioms," available to everyone. In the real world the role of an axiom is played by a "hard fact." Unfortunately, a hard fact is rare. At best, information is fuzzy; at worst, someone is distorting it.

As we model an event we try to get to the bottom of it. We hunger to know the heart of the matter, to place ourselves at ground zero of what really happened.

From time to time we are given a chance to peek into the inner sanctum. How we salivate when we hear that a microphone was left on after the speaker was sure it was safely off. Or a Freedom of Information request exposes a secretly recorded conversation, or a memorandum never intended to reach the public eye reaches the front page of the newspaper. Or an investigative reporter exposes a cover-up.

THE BULL'S EYE

We can think of an event—whether it's a terrorist act, a vote of Congress, a flood in New Orleans, a war in Iraq—as a bull's eye in a target. Surrounding this bull's eye are concentric rings. The innermost ring is the initial report. The next few rings may consist of the follow-up stories with more details. Next may come the commentaries, and later, perhaps, the rings provided by historians.

For instance, we hear that the Senate voted to approve importing of lower-cost prescription drugs. That is the first ring, the initial report. Then we learn that the bill had a poison pill amendment saying that the Secretary of Health and Human Service must certify that the drugs "pose no additional risk to the public's health and safety." Call that the second ring. The third ring is that the Secretary had already announced he would not certify such drugs. The fourth ring, hidden even further in the background, is the role of the pharmaceutical industry.

The Senators can claim that they voted to allow imports, and we laypersons would be none the wiser. And when it was all over, we would have no idea what really happened. We would be left wondering why we can import millions of doses of vaccines against a flu epidemic, yet not prescription medicines. We would have to hire a private eye to penetrate the rings. Most of us, holding down an eight-hour job and wanting to relax in the evening with our family, are already saturated. Someday a book may appear to tell us what took place.

It is as though a rock dropped into a pool sends out concentric ripples. The rock entering the water is the initial event. The ripples symbolize the layers of misinformation, rumor, secrets, and distortions that surround the event.

There is another way to view the bull's eye and the ripples. At the bull's eye are the participants in the event. Here we find the insiders, the potential whistle blowers, each of whom has firsthand knowledge of part of what happened. Then come the eyewitnesses, who were not among the actors but saw the event at a distance. Then come those who tell the story: reporters, editors, neighbors, and finally the outer rings, the general public, struggling to make an accurate model of reality. By contrast, at our job or in our home we are right at the bull's eye.

We on an outer ring go by several names, such as, "person in the street," "layperson," "outsider," and "the public." Our hard knowledge about public events is thin. We usually don't have a right to entertain an opinion about many of the flaming issues of the day. As an outsider, we tend to agree with the last insider who talked to us. In short, the foundation of our model is shallow.

A raw, unadulterated fact is rare. That may be why we are attracted by fires, accidents, and sports events. What we see there is what actually happened. Most events of interest, because they are of interest, pass through someone's prism. They are turned into mere words, with their inevitable limitations and twists. No wonder we try to get behind the curtain that blocks our view of the action.

As the commentator Thomas Friedman put it, "If there is anything I've learned as a reporter, it's that when you get away from 'the thing itself' — the core truth about a situation — you get into trouble." That means that you and I are in trouble most of the time.

PERCEPTION AND THE MODEL

I am not the first to contrast reality and appearance. Five centuries ago Machiavelli in his book *The Prince* observed that:

> *A prince need not have all the good qualities I mentioned, but he should certainly appear to have them. To those seeing and hearing him, he should appear to be a man of compassion, a man of good faith, a man of integrity, a kind and a religious man. And there is nothing so important as to seem to have this last quality. Men in general judge by their eyes rather than by their hands; because everyone is in a position to watch, few are in a position to come in close touch with you. Everyone sees what you appear to be, few experience what you really are.*

The same advice applies today, as every politician knows. Now it's much easier to implement because it is harder for us to get in close touch with our leaders, and much easier for them to use the modern media to convey a misleading image of themselves.

The Congressional leader, Newt Gingrich, exploited this naive observation. As Michael Johnson, his chief of staff, remarked:

> *He excelled at the politics of perception; it does not matter what happened on the floor of the House on any day— if you can describe it your way, you define it. He made the politics of perception into an art form.*

The first President Bush put it a little differently:

In politics, you have to remember, it isn't what's actually happening — it's the perception that's out there.

His son learned that lesson well, as we can read in David Kuo's *Tempting Faith:*

He is a good man. But he is a politician; a very smart and shrewd politician. And if the faith-based initiative was teaching me anything, it was about the president's capacity to care about perception more than reality. He wanted it to look good. He cared less about it being good.

But it is not only in politics that perception plays a key role. It should come as no surprise that the CIA and Pentagon hired a public relations consultant, John Rendon, who described himself as,

a politician, and a person who uses communication to meet public policy and corporate policy objectives. In fact, I am an information warrior and a perception manager.

We are surrounded by perception managers.

What Machiavelli, Gingrich, Bush, Kuo and Rendon say applies to everything we are exposed to. This may be an exaggeration, but it's a reasonable first approximation as we try to make sense of the world.

Reports of what happens come to us already processed. It's harder for news of an event to reach us without spin than to throw a ball without spin. Indeed, inaccuracy is as sure to creep in as it is in any attempt to show distances faithfully in a map of the round earth on a flat piece of paper,

That is why the word "scandal" in a headline tempts us to read on. So do the words "exposé", "inside information," "inside story," "the truth behind," "internal company memorandum," "smoking gun," "leak," "behind the scenes," "what really happened," and "whistle blower reveals." We hope that at last to get at least a fleeting glimpse of "truth." After all, we know that nations, corporations, and individuals wish to present themselves in a favorable light. This desire gives truth a nudge, and makes autobiographies suspect.

Who has not been taken by surprise when the "happily married" couple next door or on the other side of the wall files for divorce? Or when the "rich" neighbor with the Porsche and the designer suits files for bankruptcy?

One moment we are told the Japanese economy is a miracle, which we should imitate. The next we read it has collapsed, burdened by massive bad debts that the banks refuse to scratch off the books. One moment we hear the Mexican economy is expanding at a healthy rate, the next that it is in trouble and needs a guarantee on a loan of fifty billion dollars. To follow the news is to be buffeted by surprising, often contradictory shocks.

OUR HUNGER FOR THE TRUTH

We know that what we see is not the "naked truth," but rather, at best, a photograph that has been touched up and cropped, even with just the innocent intent of trying to convey it faithfully. Words are imprecise, easily misinterpreted, and laden with connotation. They inhabit the world of symbols, while events occur in the world of space and time.

So we are left knowing that there is the bull's eye and we are far from it. That may be the reason that the ball that Barry Bonds hit to break Hank Aaron's record of 755 home runs sold for $752,467. You can gaze at the ball and say, "Wow. This is the very ball that Bonds hit." It may look exactly like any other baseball, but it is surrounded by an authenticated halo.

The curator of an exhibition about Sigmund Freud observed that viewers want not just a copy but the genuine artifact, "People would line up to see an original document from the founding years of the United States. But put in a perfect facsimile that no one can recognize as a facsimile — if you tell people it's a facsimile, the lines disappear immediately."

On a visit to New York's Metropolitan Museum of Art, I once watched an artist copy a Frans Hals painting of a man laughing. She duplicated every brush stroke and color exactly. I couldn't tell her version from the original. To prevent such skillful copies from entering an art market bedeviled by forgeries, the Met insists that the copy should not be the same size as the original. Even so, I could imagine her gradually furnishing an entire "Museum of the Perfect Copy" matching the Met room for room. Perhaps she would place her museum in Kansas to serve those who never visit New York. Even though her paintings were to the lay eye indistinguishable from those in the Met, would anyone visit her museum? Probably not.

When Daniel Ellsberg was an insider at the Pentagon he was authorized to read documents labeled "top secret." As Henry Kissinger was about to move from the outer rings to become National Security Adviser, Ellsberg warned him that soon he would have access to vast amounts of secret information. He would feel like a fool for having "studied, written, talked about these subjects, criticized and analyzed decisions made by presidents for years without having known of the existence of all this information." Then, when he had the information, he would feel that all those who didn't were fools and he would be unable to treat what they have to say seriously. "You'll become something like a moron. You'll become incapable of learning from most people in the world." But after a while he would realize that even the secret information could be incomplete. So, even when you think you have reached the bull's eye, you may still be an outsider.

By the time a report reaches the public, it may have experienced so many changes, both intended and accidental, that no one knows what really happened. We may be left with big riddles, such as: Who is responsible for the end of the Soviet Union? Was it Gorbachev, opening up the society? Was it Reagan, with his arms buildup? Or did the Soviet Union simply implode after decades of mismanagement?

These uncertainties linger despite our access to countless websites whose total content makes the Encyclopedia Britannica look as limited as a tide table. The interpretation depends not only on the event, but also on the model in our brain—colloquially, on the axe to be ground. Maybe all the websites cancel out or get lost in their sheer numbers.

We are left with the image of the bull's eye surrounded by rings. The difficulty of reaching the bull's eye, combined with the fragility of our model, shows why we are such tempting targets, such easy pushovers.

3 Veneer

We can stop worrying; Maybe we can't;
The fog of peace.

I've called us a frivolous bunch. Now I'll justify that claim by using myself as a case study. I'm typical because once we are away from our own area of expertise we are all amateurs. The case concerns what is called "global warming" or "climate crisis."

Some say the warming is just a natural event in the long cycle of warm and cool periods. Others say that it is manmade, a consequence of our using the atmosphere as a dump ever since the start of the Industrial Revolution over two centuries ago.

What do we see? The environment getting worse—the air and water more polluted, the forests disappearing, rich farmland succumbing to urban sprawl? Or do we see things getting better—the sea lions, once almost extinct, now thriving, toxic dumps being cleaned up, and the use of solar and wind energy on the rise?

When we look at the world, as at that optical illusion in the opening chapter, what is the correct image, the axiom that will serve as the starting point?

WE CAN STOP WORRYING

My wife is very sensitive to the impact of modern civilization and population growth. If she sees a dead branch on a pine tree along the highway, she is sure the whole forest is doomed. If the rainfall is less than normal, she fears a multi-year drought has begun. A summer heat wave convinces her that global warming is already upon us and that the rising sea will in a few years inundate the very road we are traveling on.

Perhaps she is more alert than most of us, and closer to the truth. Or is she a born pessimist and the world is not as threatened as she fears? In any case, though I too am concerned about the fate of the planet, I have found her gloom hard to take. Out of self-interest I wanted to cheer her up, to assure her that the degradation of everything was not inevitable.

Then I heard that a book by Bjorn Lomborg, *The Skeptical Environmentalist*, proves that things are not getting worse but better—that forests are not shrinking, but expanding, that there is more food per person, more energy, plenty of fish, no threat from acid rain, no need to worry about getting cancer from the environment, and so on. The blurbs on the cover were enthusiastic: "At last a book that gives the environment the scientific analysis it deserves," and "A brilliant and powerful book." I decided to give her a copy. It might cheer her up. At least it would complicate her brooding.

A review in the Washington Post encouraged my hope:

The media treat the environment as a subject of cease-less decline, hastened by the indifference of ruthless capitalists and their toady politicians. But The Skeptical Environmentalist, a superbly documented and readable book by a former member of Greenpeace, has a different story to tell.

Before I gave it to my wife I browsed through its 515 pages, which were filled with dozens of tables, graphs, and illustrations. Its 25 chapters covered just about every environmental issue, such as food, waste, biodiversity, acid rain, energy, and pollution. The references and footnotes filled over 150 pages. Even the index went on for ten pages. I felt assured that this was the book to rescue my wife from her despair. What looked to me like scholarly objectivity certainly lightened my worries.

I looked forward to reading every chapter, not only to be cheered, but because I take a perverse pleasure in seeing someone challenge my beliefs. It helps keep me on my toes. (It's unfortunate that liberals tend to subscribe to liberal journals and conservatives to conservative journals. It ought to be the other way around, or at least each subscribing to a mix, to avoid going off the deep end.)

In any case, I was curious about Lomborg's book, if only to check that I wasn't in a rut.

In his preface Lomborg writes, "I'm an old left-wing Greenpeace member and for a long time had been concerned about environmental questions." But after studying the issues he concluded, "The air in the developed world is becoming less, not more, polluted; people in the developing countries are not starving more, but less, and so on." If the truth turned this left-winger around, then surely it would comfort me and convert my wife.

MAYBE WE CAN'T

Before I gave her the book, I found on the Web some disconcerting reviews of it. They condemned it for misinterpreting data and omitting references that undermined the arguments. Some . of the reviewers were even specialists quoted in the book. Here is a sample of what I found:

One review. *The reader should be wary in particular of Lomborg's passion for statistics: overarching averages can obscure a lot of important detail. One might reasonably conclude that Lomborg intentionally selects his data and citations to distort or even reverse the truth.*

Another. *In his introduction, the statistician tells us that his skills lie in 'knowing how to handle international statistics.' Later he confesses that, 'I am not myself an expert as regards environmental problems.' Unfortunately, statistical prowess does not guarantee understanding. A little more expert knowledge would have diluted this book's glib optimism. Indeed, the book would probably never have been written.*

There were more reviews with the same flavor. I was surprised and disappointed. It was embarrassing to see how easily I had been manipulated. I couldn't give the book to my wife.

A while later I learned that Lomborg had been appointed head of the Danish Institute for Environmental Assessment. That suggested that his book was objective and I could depend on it.

Months later I came upon a report of the Danish Committee on Scientific Dishonesty, a division of the Danish Research Agency, which is like our National Academy of Sciences. After a six-month review, they concluded that Lomborg's work "is deemed to fall within the concept of scientific dishonesty. It is clearly contrary to the standards of good scientific practice." They cited an extensive critique in the *Scientific American*. But Lomborg claimed that critique was biased, being the work of scientists convinced that the environment was getting worse.

A year later The Danish Ministry of Science, Technology, and Innovation announced that the panel had erred in not identifying exactly where Lomborg had been dishonest and in not giving him a chance to defend himself. Though the Ministry's criticisms were of the panel's method, not its conclusion, Lomborg asserted, "The panel's verdict cannot still be said to stand." He must have rehabilitated his reputation, because in 2006 his organization, the Copenhagen Consensus Center, ran a conference attended by eight United Nations ambassadors.

I mention this experience not to argue about the fate of the world or of Lomborg. I chose it because it is typical of so many issues. In each one our knowledge is such a thin veneer that our opinions can easily be swayed by any articulate spokesperson. On few subjects have we earned the right to have an opinion.

THE FOG OF PEACE

So we walk through life knowing a little about much. Our ignorance is symbolized by the quartz watch on our wrist. If asked how it works, we reply, "There's a quartz crystal that vibrates at a constant rate." But if asked to make the watch, we would quickly have to admit we have no real understanding of how it works. That watch reminds us how superficial is our knowledge of life outside our job and home.

We wander through the fog of peace, analogous to the more famous "fog of war." We look at the paint on our car and have no idea what makes it stay on. As a kid I thought it was the pressure of the atmosphere. And what makes glue stick? I still don't know. It's amazing that in our blissful ignorance of our immediate surroundings we make it from day to day. Our understanding of the worlds of commerce, politics, and international relations is truly pitiful. Put on the witness stand to testify on most topics, we would collapse in tears under the gentlest cross-examination.

Yet at this moment the local and global news insists that I have to have an opinion on such varied issues as solar energy, the location of a new junior high school, the fate of Tibet and Taiwan, the Middle East problem, the legal rights of gay partners, pension legislation, the effectiveness of the death penalty, prayer in the schools, a missile shield, the legalization of drugs, the causes of crime, the future of dams, abortion, the privatization of social security, the welfare system, the estate tax, and so on. This small sample of issues shows the impossibility of being a well-informed citizen. Yet it's hard to resist the temptation to react to each of these as though I had to vote on them or had to be ready to respond to a stubborn pollster who won't accept the response, "No opinion." No wonder the popularity of a president can rise and fall so quickly. We are a fickle bunch. If only we had a way to convince ourselves that we don't know enough about a subject to commit ourselves to one way or the other.

The insiders are aware of our superficiality. As David Kuo, whom I have already quoted, writes, "Our White House understood both the news cycle and America's attention span. It realized the latter was short and the former manic. The American public has a notoriously brief attention span even for major news. Within weeks even a tsunami can become old news. When it comes to politics, the vast majority of people look at headlines, watch a thirty-second story, and then move on to think about *American Idol,* dinner, or anything else more captivating."

Maybe there is a way to determine whether we are fools on a particular issue. We may pause to ask ourselves how many minutes we spent collecting the facts. If only a few, we would be foolish to offer an opinion. Another test is to notice how easily we are swayed by the last speaker to present the case on either side. If easily, then surely our knowledge is superficial.

In truth I haven't the faintest idea whether the earth is getting warmer. Computer simulations suggest that it is, but the computer's output depends on the assumptions and numbers put into it by its master. The programmer is like a ventriloquist and the computer plays the role of the dummy on his lap. Besides, I am leery of models that use many variables; I prefer to depend on calculations that can be done on the back of an envelope.

On the other hand, meteorologists report that temperatures have been rising. On the other hand, maybe such changes are natural, not man-made. On the other hand, the growing blanket of carbon dioxide may trap heat. On the other hand, dust may block the sun. The "on the other hands" could go on and on, as they do in *Fiddler on the Roof*.

We should be unsure of ourselves. We have no way to check everything. No wonder the insiders can play games with our minds.

The next two chapters describe a couple of those games.

4 Distortion by Omission

Hiding the fact; Even a president omits;
Omission is widely practiced.

In scientific research, the goal is to deepen our knowledge of the universe. That is not the goal of most of us outside the laboratory. Our objective is to accomplish a mission, whether to win a battle, make money, or implement a political program. Truth may advance the program, but so may falsehood. Truth may, on the contrary, interfere with achieving the agenda. Whoever is willing to invent credible myths has two tools at his disposal. This is as true in daily life as it is in the highest levels of government, where, according to Paul O'Neill, former Secretary of the Treasury, "Politics, as it's played, is not about being right. It's about doing whatever's necessary to win. They're not the same." Another insider reported, "Washington has become a breeding ground for deception and a killing field for truth."

One of the most effective myths helped President Reagan make his case for welfare reform. He cited the "Welfare Queen" of Chicago, who had ripped off $150,000 in benefits with the aid of eighty aliases, thirty addresses, and a dozen Social Security cards. The country was outraged.

Reporters, hoping to interview her, were frustrated until they discovered there was no such person. However, the myth should be commended, both for the imagination of its creator as well as for its effectiveness. The key to such a myth is that outsiders should believe it, that it takes awhile to be exposed, and that few will ever notice its exposure. So many myths enter the information stream that even the "urban-legends" website, with its red for false and green for true, cannot keep up with them.

In science an experiment in one lab can be repeated in other labs. If a scientist makes a claim, other scientists need not accept it on faith. Rather, they try to duplicate the experiment. The more astonishing the claim, the more convincing the experiment must be. But outside the laboratory the "experiment" can usually be done just once since the world constantly changes. Instead of experiment followed by experiment we have an event followed by rhetoric.

HIDING THE FACT

A more brutal but sometimes more effective response from someone who does not like a particular fact is simply to smother it, to hide it long enough if not forever. I call this "distortion by omission."

"Long enough" may mean, for instance, "until after the election." This clean and elegant maneuver is still possible in spite of surveillance cameras, secret tapes, monitored conversations, planted bugs, black boxes, and hard disks, to say nothing of such primitive means as the Freedom of Information Act, whistle blowers, and countless debunking websites.

A memorandum written by a Phillip Morris employee about research on the effects of smoking illustrates the technique:

> *If she is able to demonstrate no withdrawal effects of nicotine, we will pursue this avenue with vigor. If, however, the results with nicotine are similar to those gotten with morphine or caffeine, we will want to bury it.*

The study was buried for a quarter century. Would anyone expect the company to display unfavorable research on a billboard?

The practitioner of distortion by omission risks premature exposure. This was the case with stock market analysts, who would praise stocks publicly that they privately admitted were about to collapse. They just failed to mention that the stock should be avoided and that their firm had a big stake in it. Still, the technique worked for years and they kept their millions in commissions. For this reward they must have contributed something to society, perhaps giving us the thrill we experience when we scratch a lottery ticket. Gamblers are entertained at casinos, even if mathematics guarantees that in the long run most will lose.

EVEN A PRESIDENT OMITS

President Johnson provides a classic illustration of the omission technique: by the time it was exposed he was dead. In 1964, he told Congress that an attack by North Vietnamese patrol boats on our destroyers was unprovoked. In fact, it was provoked, for our navy had been supporting South Vietnamese raids on the North Vietnamese coast. Johnson exploited the attack to persuade Congress to pass the Tonkin Gulf Resolution, which gave him the authority to expand the war in Vietnam.

Some thirty years later, secretly recorded White House tapes revealed that Johnson well understood the technique of omission. We can listen in on a conversation between him and an old friend on August 4, 1964, as they discuss Vice President Hubert Humphrey.

LBJ: *"Our friend Hubert is just destroying himself with his big mouth."*

Rowe: *"Is he talking again?"*

LBJ: *"Yeah, all the time. And you just can't stop it. Yesterday he went on TV and just blabbed everything that he had heard in a briefing. They said, 'How would you account for those PT boat attacks on our destroyers when we are innocently out there in the gulf, sixty miles from shore?' Humphrey said, 'Well, we've been carrying out some operations in that area, going and knocking out roads and petroleum things.' And that is exactly what we have been doing."*

Rowe: *"Good Lord!"*

LBJ: *"The damned fool just ought to keep his goddamned big mouth shut on foreign affairs...He's hurting the government. And he's hurting us."*

Even though Humphrey had blurted out the secret on TV, Johnson was able to control the damage and escalate the war.

This technique of omission or secrecy is not limited to one political party. All insiders must know that it is quite easy to bamboozle us laypersons, who live far from the bull's eye. According to Scott McClellan, press secretary for the second President Bush, that White House engaged in "spin, stonewalling, hedging, evasion, denial, noncommunication, and deceit by omission." But just the one word, "omission," encompasses all those techniques.

In 1970, Salvador Allende was elected president of Chile. Reading the news, I assumed that our government would be happy, for democracy was spreading in Latin America. Imagine my surprise when this CIA memorandum surfaced three decades later:

> *When one considers Allende's superb political performance during the first two months of his administration, and the speed and effectiveness with which the UP [Allende's party] has moved to implement the most popular aspects of its program, it becomes obvious that the UP goal of a popular electoral majority may be achieved in the April elections. Such a victory could encourage nascent popular unity movements elsewhere in the hemisphere...*

What a naive fool I had been thirty years earlier. For three years, our government schemed to undermine that democracy. Finally, in 1973, it succeeded in replacing Allende with a dictator, Pinochet.

When there were wide protests against the atrocities of the Pinochet death squads in Chile, I assumed that our government was trying to persuade him to stop murdering critics of his regime.

As with Allende, thirty years later I learned that I was wrong. The book *The Pinochet Papers*, based on CIA and other long-secret documents, revealed that our government believed that human rights do not mix well with foreign policy. In closed meetings with Chilean officials, Secretary of State Kissinger brushed aside such concerns with the following:

> *I read the briefing paper and it was nothing but human rights. The State Department is made up of people who have a vocation for the ministry. Because there are not*

*enough churches for them, they went into the Depart-
ment of State.*

Before he gave a speech on the importance of human rights he privately assured the officials that his remarks did not apply to them.

We laypersons are so far from the bull's eye that insiders can easily tinker with our perceptual options and our flimsy models. That the government misleads us mocks the foundation of a democracy. How can a voter, an outsider such as you or I, who is denied the truth, cast a ballot based on thoughtful deliberation? If this is the practice, how can we claim that every nation should become a democracy modeled on ours?

OMISSION IS WIDELY PRACTICED

In 1961, Yuri Gagarin became the first human in space, sweeping out one orbit of the earth in 108 minutes. The Soviet space agency reported his flight as flawless. Only in 1996 did it become widely known that Gagarin almost died during the descent. For ten minutes, his capsule spun out of control. Revealing this promptly could have slowed down both the Russian and American space programs. Omission, the opposite of disclosure, does have its uses.

Similarly, during World War I, newspapers in Great Britain were not allowed to show photographs of dead British soldiers, presumably so as not to undermine support for the war. The firing squad was the penalty for anyone caught violating the order. As the Vietnam War demonstrated, showing such photos can help end a war. It was prudent of our leaders to go one step further during the occupation of Iraq, and not permit even photos of flag-draped coffins. As Senator Hiram Johnson observed in 1917, "The first casualty when war comes is truth." The more remote the bull's eye, the easier it is to control information about it. This is especially so of bull's eyes in foreign lands, not just a war, but, say, the efficiency of medical care.

Just by reading the daily newspaper, we can easily extend this list. It's prudent to assume distortion by omission is present. However, it is not enough to read "between the lines." To protect ourselves from distortion by omission, we are obliged to imagine missing pages or entire books not yet written, and miles of shelves holding documents marked "classified."

The slogan, "The first casualty in peace is truth" may help us stay alert. Though it may exaggerate the extent of intentional corrupting of our models, it may not be much of a stretch. In any case, it will remind us to get our information from varied sources, even from those that offend our model of the world.

DISTORTION BY OMISSION

U.S. Withheld Data Showing Driving Risks

Merrill Bonus Details Ordered To Be Disclosed

U.S. Withheld Data on Cellphone Driving Risks

Judge Finds Pricewaterhouse Withheld Data

Judge Says Figures Don't Constitute a Trade Secret

Secret's Out: Swiss Bank To Disclose Some Clients

Senate Backs Ban on Photos Of G.I. Coffins

Defense Chief Lifts Ban On Pictures of Coffins

Chemical Company Withheld Information About Explosion

Doubts on Informant Deleted in Senate Text

Undisclosed Losses at Merrill Lead to a Trading Inquiry

Results of Drug Trials Can Mystify Doctors Through Omission

Leisure World Panel Says It Will Sue to Keep Books Secret

5 Distortion by Commission

Commision; Even the suspicious can be fooled;
Dumping a politician; The case of Libya;
What's in a name?

Nothing in the world of mathematics prepared me to deal with the techniques insiders use for manipulating my model of what is true and what is false. Intentionally misleading people is not a crime unless done under oath or in a financial transaction. The goal in real life is to win, as I quoted O'Neill observing. It is not to discover a new theorem or to obtain a fresh insight into the human condition or into the nature of the universe.

COMMISSION

Omission has the same advantage as arson: well done, it leaves no trace. The opposite technique, commission, though more common, lacks this advantage. In this approach one tries to distort our model by whatever means that seem promising. It could be an outright lie, or just some misleading statement that throws dust in our eyes. In its subtlest form, it is accompanied by adroit omissions.

Pentagon planners make this explicit in their description of perception management, which it defines as "actions to convey and (or) deny selected information ... to foreign audiences to influence their emotions, motives, and objective reasoning ..."

It is even possible to commit and omit at the same time. One standard way to accomplish this is to dribble out bad news so slowly, over so many days, that no one notices it. It doesn't reach the threshold of being important.

When President Johnson was vastly increasing the number of our troops in Vietnam, he was advised, "in order to mitigate somewhat the crisis atmosphere that would result from this major U. S. action . . . announcements about it be made piecemeal . . .," advice that he followed. Big banks dribble out the bad news of their horrific losses bit by bit as if they had no idea how miserable their balance sheet was.

Another method is to release bad news Friday afternoon, preferably just before a holiday weekend, giving it time to get lost while everyone is recuperating from a hard workweek. According to California Representative Mike Thompson this is what happened when it was discovered that the federal budget deficit was $200 billion more than had been announced two months earlier. As he warned, "Unfortunately, it's typical for this administration to release this type of unflattering news on a Friday afternoon." To be well informed, we should be especially alert on Fridays.

But we can be massaged so subtly that we aren't aware of being influenced. It took me a long time to notice that almost every commercial has a music background, sometimes as loud as the words. Evidently, someone had figured out that the music would lull me into believing the message.

Recently oil companies have been running full-page ads identifying themselves as "energy companies," ready to supply me with solar, wind, and geothermal energy. This is as absurd as if the manufacturer of my dining room table announced that it would meet all my dining needs, plates, silverware, tablecloth, and napkins. For reasons they don't reveal they evidently want to corner the energy market, not necessarily to my benefit.

When President Reagan appeared on television, the stage was carefully set to persuade us to like him. In particular, the chairs were selected for their rounded arms. I learned that only years later. It's hard to protect ourselves from such subtle maneuvers. Evidently we have to pay as much attention to the background, to the visible, as to the words. That includes the little American flag pins that politicians must display on their lapels. What are they trying to say to me? That "I'm more patriotic than the other guy?" That's not the message I receive. Instead I'm reminded of that aphorism, "Patriotism is the last refuge a scoundrel." In any case, we have to watch out for the subliminal, for that is where the main action may well be going on.

When American dignitaries visited Baghdad during the occupation those standing near them were asked not to wear helmets and body armor, for such protection would appear to contradict claims that military victory was near. I learned this much later, long after the ruse had achieved its goal. How was I to know in real time that someone was playing with my mind?

EVEN THE SUSPICIOUS CAN BE FOOLED

I will illustrate distortion by commission with an example that also shows how hard it is to move from an outer ring to get behind the scene and approach the epicenter. It concerns Sol Wachtler, once chief judge of the state of New York.

While serving as a judge, Wachtler visited several prisons, including Attica and Sing Sing, to show inmates that "he cared about their conditions." That seemed a wise move, since a judge should know what happens when he sentences a person to serve time. He was no fool: "I knew that I saw only what I was supposed to see, but I felt my visit was a demonstration to the inmates that I cared."

Unfortunately for him, he became infatuated with a woman whom he eventually harassed. Displeased by such attention, she brought charges, and he found himself behind bars. There at the epicenter he saw how the tours for visiting judges were conducted:

> How deluded I was by my own vanity and by those escorts who so carefully planned my itinerary. The visitors were shown a part of the mental health unit that was air-conditioned and comparatively spacious. They were not escorted through the vast majority of the units, which were unventilated, cramped, double-bunked cells built for two but each holding four inmates. The guards are on their best behavior, and troublesome inmates are

> *tucked away in some remote locale. The TV cabinets,*
> *always padlocked, are miraculously opened. The meals*
> *are actually edible.*

The prison officials were practicing a mix of omission by not showing some parts, and commission, by spiffing up others.

Getting the nation to support the Iraq war also involved the same mix. It was sold the same way a good salesman sells a sofa or a car: speak only of the benefit and don't mention the cost. The goal of the administration was to keep everyone "on message." However, the president's chief economic advisor, Larry Lindsey, blurted out that the war would cost between $100 and $200 billion. Scott McClellan, who saw all this from the inside, reported later,

> *None of the unpleasant consequences of war – casualties,*
> *economic effects, geopolitical risks, diplomatic repercus-*
> *sions - were part of the message. We were in campaign*
> *mode ... Lindsey's transgression could only make the war*
> *harder to sell ... Within four months, Larry was gone,*
> *having "resigned."*

The technique of commission and omission worked: most of us laypersons made no effort to seek another source of information.

DUMPING A POLITICIAN

The same technique removed a politician who had been making trouble for the hog farmers of North Carolina. In the two decades beginning in 1980, hog farming there had rapidly expanded to become the leading agricultural producer in the state. No laws prevented the waste from fouling the air and polluting the streams and drinking water. Representative Cindy Watson said, "This is wrong, what you guys are doing, those big hog people. Some of you helped elect me but I can't do what you want me to do," and in 1997 she helped pass a moratorium to limit the growth of hog farms until the industry could find a better way to get rid of its waste.

This displeased the hog farmers, who formed a group that collected over two million dollars and launched a yearlong campaign of ads and phone calls to get rid of Watson. It was not called "Hog

Farmers Who Want to Continue Despoiling the Environment."
Instead it was named "*Farmers for Fairness.*"

The phone solicitors did not say, "Do you know Watson is
trying to regulate the hog industry in order to protect the environment?" Instead they said, "She often doesn't get her facts right,"
or, "She flip-flops on issues," or, "She misleads people about her
record on the environment." This campaign to destroy Watson's
reputation succeeded: she lost the Republican primary to a hog
farmer.

We may be amused by a group that consists mainly of large
corporations calling themselves *"Farmers for Fairness,"* but a
name is a serious matter. Most of us are so busy keeping our nose
above water that we don't have the time to wonder, "Who is really
behind this name?" nor have we the money with which to hire a
detective to find out. The sponsors of a TV political ad are listed
at the end, but so briefly and in such light print, that, as intended,
we have no chance to read it.

A falsehood repeated often enough turns into a truth but a
truth repeated often enough may degenerate into a mere truism.
The cry, "the liberal press," has been shouted so long that we
believe that the press has a liberal slant. Such is the power of
distortion by repeated commission. Even some conservatives
admit that the press does not have a liberal bias. As Rich Bond,
then chair of the Republican Party, said in 1992, "There is some
strategy to it [bashing the 'liberal' media.] If you watch any great
coach, what they try to do is 'work the refs.' Maybe the ref will cut
you a little slack on the next one." Patrick Buchanan, a conservative presidential candidate, acknowledged, "I've gotten balanced
coverage. For heaven sakes, we kid about the 'liberal' media,' but
every Republican does that." The book, *What Liberal Media?*, by
Eric Alterman, even argues that there is a bias in the news, but it
favors the conservatives.

THE CASE OF LIBYA

Almost every day, when I read the newspaper I am reminded how
gullible I am and how convincing is the deft one-two punch of
omission and commission. I'll give a typical example.

On December 19, 2003, the second President Bush announced that Colonel Qaddafi had decided to end Libya's efforts to obtain weapons of mass destruction. Three weeks later, on January 12, 2004, William Safire's column explained Qaddafi's thinking:

> Qaddafi took one look at our army massing for the invasion of Iraq and decided to get out of the mass-destruction business... The notion that the terror-supporting dictator's epiphany was not the direct result of our military action, but of decade-long diplomatic pleas for goodness and mercy, is laughable.

Since Safire also wrote a fascinating column on words, I knew he was a smart man, who wouldn't be easily fooled. His explanation convinced me, shaping my model of the world.

On January 20, the President, in his State of the Union address, confirmed my view:

> Nine months of intense negotiations ... succeeded with Libya, while 12 years of diplomacy with Iraq did not. And one reason is clear: For diplomacy to be effective, words must be credible and no one can now doubt the word of America.

Now I had no doubt that our action in Iraq had frightened Qaddafi into cooperating.

But three days, later I happened upon an op-ed piece by Flynt Leverett in the *New York Times*, headlined, "Why Libya Gave Up the Bomb." Though I felt I already knew why, I read it after seeing that the author had served as a senior director for Middle Eastern affairs at the National Security Council from 2002 to 2003 — which put him near the bull's eye. He pointed out that "carrot-and-stick" negotiations going back to the Clinton administration had methodically produced regular progress. Growing out of those negotiations, in the spring of 2003, Libya proposed dismantling its weapons program:

> The Iraq war, which had not yet started, was not the driving force behind Libya's move. Rather, Libya was willing to deal because of credible diplomatic representations by the United States over the years....

Now I believed Leverett's explanation. I felt that Safire and the president had hoodwinked me. By commission — emphasizing the Iraq war — and by omission — not mentioning the years of successful negotiations, they controlled my thinking. Fortunately, since I am just an outsider, in no position to shape world events, I felt no harm was done.

"However," as Leverett pointed out, "by linking shifts in Libya's behavior to the Iraq war, the president misrepresents the real lesson of the Libya case. This confusion undermines our chances of getting ... Iran and Syria to follow Libya's lead." The key to success with Libya was a mixture of carrots and sticks, with the carrots playing a big role.

At the bull's eye was Qaddafi himself. I wonder what he would say if I asked him why he changed his mind. Unfortunately, he may not give the reason, out of a desire not to irritate even an ex-president.

WHAT'S IN A NAME?

Environmental issues provide a fertile source of cleverly chosen titles for groups that oppose legislation intended to preserve natural resources. For instance, *The National Wilderness Institute* brings to mind bald eagles and hikers wandering in snowy mountains. In fact it is a group formed to roll back wetlands regulation in the Endangered Species Act.

What comes to mind when we encounter "*The Wilderness Impact Research Foundation*"? Probably some biologists carrying butterfly nets into the forest. Wrong. It is an organization of loggers and ranchers who want to exploit the wilderness. I admire their imagination and would like to have eavesdropped as they chose the name.

It goes on and on. *The American Environmental Foundation* is concerned with the rights of private property. In spite of its clear-cut purpose it did not dub itself "*The People for the Preservation of Private Property*," though that has a pleasant alliterative ring. *The Global Climate Coalition* is an association of corporations resisting regulations to reduce global warming. The aim of "*Northwesterners for More Fish*" is to defeat a movement that claims that utilities, aluminum companies, and the timber industry are destroying fish habitats.

The title "*Citizens for Statewide Smoking Restrictions*" suggests a grass roots group that wishes to put more places off limits to smokers. Actually the main "citizen" was Philip Morris, which spent over twelve million dollars in a campaign for a measure that would override local anti-smoking laws in California. No one would expect the group to be called "*Tobacco Companies that Want to Sell More Cigarettes.*"

The most delightful name I've come across is *Families Associated for Inalienable Rights.* This designated a group of bankers, oilmen, realtors, and cattlemen who won repeal of a provision to increase the tax on the top three percent of estates. Even their acronym, FAIR, appeals to the casual observer. In a contest for imaginative names of groups, this would take the prize, especially if extra points were awarded for clever acronyms.

I could go on and on. It seems that nothing is what it seems. The *Hospitality Coalition for Indoor Air Quality* wants to eliminate indoor smoking bans. The *Save Our Species Alliance* would like to reduce the scope of the Endangered Species Act. But I will stop here.

Because such deceptions are common, we may wonder, once again, whether we should insist that the rest of the world practice our form of democracy.

Politicians are just as sensitive as corporations in their choice of words. They need to be; otherwise, their careers would be doomed. As Tom Donahue, President of the United States Chamber of Commerce, said, "The first one that gets the right phrase on the argument usually has the moral high ground."

It should not come as a surprise that what Democrats call the "estate tax" Republicans, who want to get rid of it, call the "death tax." Jack Faris of the National Federation of Independent Businesses commented, "Whoever the father [of the new name] was, God bless him. It has really helped us shape the debate on the unfairness of the tax, not who is paying for it."

The Democrats' "tax cuts" become the Republicans' "tax relief," with its silent connotation of a tax burden, and their "affirmative action" turns into the Republicans' "quotas and preferences." Such pairings also take place elsewhere, as in the abortion issue, with its "pro life" and "pro choice" opponents.

That clever phrase, "tax relief," reminds me how vulnerable we outsiders are to persuasion by repetition. For a century we have been told that we are overtaxed. In the Congressional Record of August 5, 1909, during the debate on whether to establish a personal income tax, I came across this remark of Senator Dick: "We hear much concerning the overburdened taxpayers of this country, yet our taxes are lower and more easily borne than those of any other civilized government." We still hear the claim that we are overburdened, followed by the same predictable rebuttal. I suspect that claim and response, with only slight changes in the wording, will be repeated as long as there are taxes.

That we are sensitive to the choice of names shows how vulnerable we are to those who want to bend our minds and revise our models. It is easy to pull us by our noses right or left, up or down. If we have any doubt how easily led we are, consider our reaction when a pollster posed these two questions about how to treat the surplus in the Federal budget:

Should the money be used for a tax cut, or should it be used to fund new government programs?

The response was sixty percent for the cut.

Then the question was put this way:

Should the money be used for a tax cut, or should it be spent on programs for education, the environment, health care, crime-fighting, and military defense?

Suddenly only twenty-two percent favored the cut, yet the question, in essence, had not changed.

Of course, where there is distortion by commission you can be on the lookout for distortion by omission, but you won't be able to see it. Soon after American troops reached Baghdad the image of Iraqis toppling a statue of Saddam Hussein in Firdos Square was flashed around the world, persuading viewers that the populace was happy to see us. In fact, there were only some two hundred Iraqis in the almost empty square. Demonstrations by thousands asking us to leave Baghdad, nine day later, were not shown.

All this chicanery makes me wonder how much substance backs up our opinions. Are they no more solid than our views in Chapter One of the thirty lines as cubes, or parallelograms, or a star, which so easily change with a blink of our eyes? Knowing that someone is using the tricks of omission and commission may help us defend ourselves. For those who want to trick us, however, manipulating our world model is their daytime job, and they get paid for their work. We are forced to uncover their tricks in our spare time and at our own expense.

Like a boxer, we have to be on guard for the right-left combination punches of omission and commission. Even if we expose them long after they have done their work, we at least have the pleasure of revealing how they did it.

6 The Art of No Opinion

The death penalty; No opinion.

Are we outsiders destined to play the role of helpless fools when it comes to the big issues? I'm not a fool in matters of algebra, geometry, and calculus, but I feel like one even on an issue as important as the "Middle East." I wonder whether I have the right to have an opinion on this matter.

In Chapter One I mentioned the two opposing views on why so many in the Middle East hate America. Both couldn't be right because the world is not that bizarre. That bothered me. I wanted to settle it one way or the other. Not because I expected a phone call from the White House asking for advice, but partly out of curiosity and partly because I live in a democracy.

In The 9/11 Commission Report I read that militants in the Middle East wish "to rid the world of religious and political pluralism, the plebiscite, and equal rights for women," hence try to attack the United States.

But in *Imperial Hubris,* a book by Michael Scheuer, a CIA analyst and chief of the Counter Terrorist Center's Osama bin Laden station, I came upon a completely different explanation: "The fundamental flaw in our thinking about Bin Laden is that 'Muslims hate and attack us for what we are and think, rather than what we do.' Muslims are bothered by our modernity . . . but they are rarely spurred to action unless American forces encroach on their lands."

I have to form my model of that part of the world only on the basis of what I read. Now I didn't know what to believe. Finally, I asked an acquaintance who had lived in the Middle East which side was right. He replied, "What does the name Mossadegh mean to you?" The name did not ring a bell. "In that case, there's a good book that will end your confusion. It's *All the Shah's Men*," which told how secret agents of Great Britain and the United States overthrew the democratically elected Iranian prime minister in 1953. I read it and it did. But there is always the chance that another book will come out and refute that one. It's not easy to approach the bull's eye, when even those who should have a clear view disagree.

My second example of the difficulty of building a solid model is more complicated: the much-discussed question of whether capital punishment deters would-be murderers.

THE DEATH PENALTY

I am typical of most people in that I had never studied the subject. I probably had spent only a few minutes reading op-ed pieces on it. My opinion, based on nothing more than instinct, was that the death penalty is not a deterrent. I reached this conclusion by the Stanislavsky method, borrowed from the training of actors. In this method, the actor is asked to "pretend that you are a fire hydrant or the King of England or whatever." When I pretended to contemplate committing a murder, I felt I could get away with it. I didn't worry about the possible penalty. Besides, if I were caught and convicted, the odds were small that my punishment would be death.

So when I came across a column in the *Boston Globe* that argued that the presence of the death penalty cut the number of homicides, I was surprised.

Jeff Jacoby, in *The Cost of a Death-Penalty Moratorium*, made a persuasive case. His reasoning seemed simple and irrefutable. From 1965 to 1980 there were almost no executions.

The data are brutal: during that period the number of murders per year skyrocketed from 9,960 to 23,040.

We might respond that the population of the country grew also. But that turns out not to explain the rise. The author had anticipated my quibble.

The murder rate — homicides per 100,000 persons — doubled from 5.1 to 10.2. Perhaps murder becomes more attractive when potential killers know that prison is the worst outcome they can face.

That was persuasive, but I wasn't totally convinced. I couldn't imagine a potential murderer saying to himself, "Before I do the deed, I'd better check what jurisdiction I'm in. I don't mind spending the rest of my life locked up watching daytime TV, but I don't want to die prematurely. Ah-ha, I see it doesn't have the death penalty, so I'll bump off my wife's lover."

Then I looked at what happened after 1980. By 1985, the murder rate had dropped to 7.9. But in 1991, it rose to 9.8, almost what it was back in 1980. Then, it gradually dropped to 5.7 in 1999 and to 5.6 in 2001.

Still curious, I looked up more information and found a table that contrasted the murder rates in states with death penalty with the rates in states without it. Oddly, in states with the penalty the murder rate for the years 1980 to 1995 was about 50 percent higher than in the "abolitionist states."

But that isn't the end of the story. It was pointed out to me that the death penalty is generally introduced in states where its citizens possess a greater urge to murder.

As I was trying to make sense of all this, two studies came out confirming the salutary effect of the death penalty. One calculated that each execution saves the lives of five victims. However, the margin of error was plus or minus ten. So one execution saves anywhere from nobody to fifteen people. Another study, this by economists, reached a similar conclusion, "A potential criminal looks at expected costs and benefits and behaves accordingly." They found that for every three pardons, there was one additional homicide.

By now, sitting high in the bleachers, I was sure that the threat of executions deterred murder. Then came a new and complicating twist into the tale. It turned out that a quantitative investigation, just like the recent ones, had been undertaken by another economist, Isaac Ehrlich, a quarter century earlier. It had reached the same verdict as those recent studies.

However, it had been roasted by other researchers, who pointed to factors that muddied the picture. "The proportion of the population residing in abolitionist states was far from uniform during the 1933-1969 period." Also, "Some of his models suggested a deterrent effect but some did not. He emphasized the models that did." The critics concluded, after pointing out other complicating considerations, "the noted difficulties render the results highly suspect."

The book, *The Death Penalty in America,* published in 1997, asserted, "Death penalty researchers have found virtually no support for the argument that the level of use of capital punishment influences murder rates."

How can researchers carry out these studies that cover decades, when the world changes so quickly? Unemployment, which breeds robberies that may involve murder, rises and falls. The prison population grows until it reaches some two million, enough to fill a large city. That probably took some would-be murderers off the streets. With all these changing influences in the society, I don't see how the scholars can reach a clear-cut conclusion. This is especially so when they have to resort to sophisticated statistical formulas to spot a trend. I certainly would not want to be in their field.

Besides, there are all sorts of murders. The *Uniform Crime Reports* lists some twenty types. Those connected with "gangland killings" are probably premeditated. But "romantic triangle," "brawl," or "argument" suggest a spontaneity impervious to the calm weighing of penalties. These three types account for almost a third of murders.

After all this, what am I to think? Will even the new studies be torn to shreds as other researchers get a close look at them?

Well, I can still say that an execution of the culprit brings "closure" to the victim's friends and relatives. But even this can be debated. If they knew that the only penalty is life imprisonment without parole, then the announcement by the jury foreman, "We find the defendant guilty as charged," would determine the moment of closure. I confess, however, that I don't know what closure means, for the agony will never end. It will only gradually diminish under the healing hand of time.

But President George W. Bush believes that the death penalty is a deterrent. I heard him say this in a debate with Vice President Gore, who agreed. Perhaps they know something that I don't know. Or maybe they don't and were just afraid of seeming to be soft on crime.

But — and there are many *buts* in this matter — what about the execution of innocent people? DNA evidence has rescued over two hundred convicts from prison. That suggests innocent people have been executed.

Just as in the preceding chapter, I've been shaken from side to side like a rag doll. That's the fate of us outsiders. Perhaps one way to approach the question is to ask prisoners on death row or even everyone convicted of homicide, "When you committed the murder did you think about the penalty — whether it was life imprisonment or death?" Their answers should help clarify matters. After all, they were at the bull's eye of the event.

All this ambiguity makes mathematics yet more appealing. As I investigate a problem I don't have to worry about the whole world. I suspect that physicists, chemists, and microbiologists must know the same delight. We can all isolate the one factor we want to look at and exclude everything else.

NO OPINION

Though polls offer the option of "No opinion," it is usually chosen by only a few participants. For those of us in the outer ring, our response to most polls ought to be "I haven't the faintest idea" or "I don't know enough to have the right to an opinion." Our morning prayer might be, "May I practice the art of 'No opinion' on subjects where I am an utter ignoramus." That raises the question of how we decide we are utter ignoramuses. We are not inclined to give ourselves such an unflattering label.

Imagine that before we vote we have to take a quiz with such questions as: "How did the United States become the only country to tie health insurance to place of employment?" or "Who was

Mossadegh?" Our score would then determine how much our vote counts. How would we suckers, used to being led by the nose, do?

In the meantime I'll try to have no opinion on the death penalty. I don't plan to murder anyone. If I did, I don't know which I would view as the stronger deterrent, a life locked up in a cage or death by lethal injection.

To develop the art of having no opinion on a controversial issue must be like seeking detachment in some Eastern religions. Having no opinion could be viewed as a religious experience. Of course, you and I are "only human," the standard apology by the species that also views itself as the most advanced creation of evolution or of the hand of God. More realistically, we could settle for this less demanding morning mantra, "I could be wrong," repeated often enough so that we would believe it.

In a democracy we are expected to have an opinion on just about everything. We are urged to go to the polls and express ourselves. That half the registered voters don't vote may simply be a sign that they are already practicing the art of no opinion. Maybe they added up the minutes they had been exposed to the cases for and against and concluded that the sum was so small that they felt unqualified to register their opinion.

Having no opinion goes against our urge to impose order on what we see. I try to suppress that urge but it's like holding my breath when my lungs demand air. Still, divers have trained themselves to hold their breath for over four minutes. The first few minutes in abstaining from having an opinion on everything are the hardest. After they pass, one is free to focus on a few key topics.

7 The Dead-Fish Principle

The principle; Examples.

At the center of the alleged fact, we may expect to find, if not a void, the vested interest: money, power, or ideology. In human affairs the "fact" is a telltale sign of action, hence of the presence of an interested party — perhaps at the center of the stage, perhaps hidden in the wings. Most likely the fact has been selected, packaged, and tied with a ribbon to further a cause. It is not the research report of an unworldly scientist, but of a worldly mortal in pursuit of a worldly goal.

A "fact" in a controversy may be suspect for two reasons, as we saw: either it is conspicuous, a fruit of commission, being pushed, or it is inaccessible, a fruit of omission, being hidden.

THE PRINCIPLE

It is only a small step from the recognition of these strong distorting forces to a belief in the dead-fish principle: Human Reality is Like a Dead Fish: the closer you get to it, the worse it smells. This may sound crude, but it is just another form of the adage, "Put your best foot forward," which can be rephrased in the negative as, "Keep your worst foot back," of which the dead-fish principle is just a more vivid version.

The dead-fish principle applies to the relation between an outsider and a bureaucracy. It would be cynical to say it applies to person-to-person relations as well, and I am of too jovial a disposition to be cynical. In those relations a neutral phrase is preferable. Erving Goffman, in his book, *The Presentation of Self in Everyday Life*, suggested the contrast between the "front of the stage" and "backstage." He presented many examples to show what we all know: we behave differently in public than in private, and that what we reveal or hide depends on who our "audience" is.

If the name "dead fish" offends, call it the "billboard" principle. One side of a billboard offers a carefully crafted message, designed to persuade. The other side, the one we are not supposed to see, is just gray unfinished wood.

To apply this principle, assume the opposite of what you are told and also that most of what you need to know is concealed. These twin assumptions serve as a simple, first approximation to the truth, as a protective knee-jerk reaction. They may turn out to be wrong, but they will keep you alert. As the saying goes, "It is better to err on the side of caution." A few examples will show how to apply the principle.

EXAMPLES

· When airlines were being urged to provide non-smoking areas in planes, government officials received many letters in opposition. Was this a sign of a grass roots rebellion? A practitioner of the dead-fish principle would say, "No, something is fishy," and then try to pry behind the scene. If persistent, he would discover this internal memorandum, prepared by the general counsel of a tobacco company:

"Attached are five drafts of 'letters' to the Civil Aeronautics Board opposing the rule to segregate smokers. Could you get some of the agency people to write these — by hand — on non-company letterheads, using home addresses, and ask each one to get one or two more, similar, but not exactly the same."

Note the quotes around "letters," an example of our theme that quotes belong around much of what we call "reality."

> · Several years later, a proposition to control smoking in public places appeared on the California ballot. An organization called "Californians for Common Sense" materialized and sponsored messages from "the folks at Californians for Common Sense" in opposition.

Applying the dead-fish principle, I went over to the Fair Elections Commission in nearby Sacramento to see who these Californians were. I was not surprised to learn that for months the group consisted only of five tobacco companies, of which the one closest to California had headquarters in Kentucky. Through the entire campaign ninety-nine percent of its funds came from those companies, local tobacco warehouses, and distributors.

Only by practicing, going behind the curtain, peeking at the back of the billboard, can we master the dead-fish principle. That is how we master any skill, whether it's playing the guitar, solving equations, or in this case, detecting signs of distortion by omission and commission.

> · Imagine that a letter arrives asking for a donation to a good cause. Is it simply what it appears to be, signed in the first person, with a handwritten note at the end? Does that mean someone who knows you signed it and wrote the note? Of course not.

The letter came out of a computer. The paper is rough. Does that mean that the charity runs a lean campaign? No. Fund-raising specialists know that such paper draws a better response than a slick look. You mail a check for fifty dollars. Does that mean the charity gets fifty dollars? No. At least half could go to a fund-raising firm. Note, incidentally, that the failure to mention this is a distortion by omission.

Charities have a tough time raising funds. No wonder some of them follow this advice in the classic *Lesly's Handbook of Public Relations and Communication*:

> *Paper, letterhead, and envelope should be of an appealing color, style, size, and quality. Each envelope should be addressed to look almost exactly like an original*

handling. The effect is reduced by a printed postage
permit used instead of a stamp. Even the style of fold-
ing is important. The standard twice-horizontal folding
is usually best.

This is a fine and harmless example of distortion by commission, an occasion for a smile rather than a frown, but still a chance to apply the dead-fish principle. Now that one can earn a masters degree in fund raising, we can expect even more sophisticated appeals.

> · Imagine that you are waiting in an auditorium for the
> candidate to arrive. He is half an hour late and the audi-
> ence is much too large for the room. A naive observer
> may say, "The candidate is unavoidably delayed and a far
> bigger crowd turned out than expected." Such a thought
> marks the neophyte.

The master would instead conclude that the crowd was assembled half an hour early and jammed into this small room to make the candidate look good, especially on TV. This analysis would be confirmed by the confidential manual, the "playbook" used by the advance party:

All handbill announcements shall show the candidate's
arrival time as thirty minutes prior to the time you know
he is scheduled to arrive. Don't worry if the room is too
small. If they're hanging from the rafters, the press will
be impressed.

Nor would he be surprised to read in the manual,

Collect all scraps of paper and other garbage from any
room used by the candidate and his entourage. Report-
ers have been known to turn up embarrassing items in
garbage cans.

Instead the master would smile, accepting both the advance men and the reporters as fellow masters of the dead-fish principle. To him, as to Shakespeare, the world is a stage, and the success of those who stand before him requires that they keep him in his seat and not let him sneak backstage.

However, even if we try to maintain our alertness to bam-boozlement at a high level, it is impossible to catch each trick.

· When dead-fish masters read that "92 million Americans will receive an average tax cut of $1083," they do not immediately go on a shopping spree. Instead, they think to themselves, "Beware of averages, for an average of a bunch of numbers is an ideal place to hide a number." They insist on finding out the original numbers: how big a tax cut the rich, the upper-middle, the middle, the lower-middle, and the poor will get.

They will learn that the 92 million omits the 50 million who get nothing. Then they will discover that half of the families get less than $100, and the majority, less than $500.

Then how could the average tax cut be $1083? The same way that the average wealth of a dozen homeless people and Bill Gates sitting around a table is half a billion dollars. A dead-fish master, rather than being angry at the deception, would get a good laugh out of the trick.

We typical outsiders do not have the time or energy to uncover the finagling behind a number, such as $1083. After a day's work, a long commute, and an update on local murders and fires, as well as trying to keep up with the marriages, divorces, weight gains and losses of celebrities, we are ready for bed, not for a research project. Whoever offered that figure, $1083, knows our limitations. The field is not level. We have to be cynical and still keep our sense of humor.

Though a poet has warned us that we can bear only so much reality, it is also true that we can bear only so much falsehood. For this reason it may be wise to apply the dead-fish principle in moderation.

CHOICE

8 The Incomparables

Apples and oranges; Society chooses;
The whole produce section; The plan and the planet.

We don't try to make sense of the world just as an exercise to keep our brain sharp. Life is not a seminar. We must also act. Before we can act we must decide between one course of action and another. We must compare and choose.

I once hoped that I could bring mathematics to bear to help make choices "rationally." Wouldn't it be wonderful if we could just make a table of benefits and costs, put a number on each item, add up the numbers, and then know what is the best course of action? I tried but finally gave up. In this and the next few chapters I will show why there is a limit to our "rationality." In fact, after looking at real decisions made in real time, including my own, I am unable to define the word "rational."

The choice may be so simple that it is effortless. For instance, our choice may be between buying gasoline for $2.79 a gallon at one station and the same gas for $2.99 at a nearby station. We just compare the two numbers and choose the station with the lower price.

But there may be complications. Perhaps there is a line of cars waiting at the cheaper station. Or maybe that station is across the street and we must cross traffic. To complicate matters even more, perhaps that company violates human rights or despoils the environment. So now the choice isn't settled just by the comparison of two numbers.

APPLES AND ORANGES

The quantitative approach has its limits. In most choices numbers don't help. These choices reduce to the "apples versus oranges" or more complex "apples versus oranges versus bananas" questions. Just how the choice is made is a mysterious process, which I leave for psychologists to explore. My goal now is more modest.

I want only to illustrate how common are the choices between incomparables. They surround us, just as radio waves do. They are so frequent that we don't notice them. I will present several cases, from the level of the individual, namely me, up through public choices.

I'll start with my own experience.

· Do I open the window to let in fresh air or close it to keep out the traffic noise? The answer may depend on how noisy the traffic and how stuffy the indoor air. I'm left comparing noise and stuffiness. Not easy, but somehow I do make the comparison. More precisely, I either open or close the window. I cannot leave it partially open in a compromise that reflects the difficulty of reaching a decision. Between the time the question arises and the time I act there is a gap that occurs when I seem to do the impossible: compare incomparables.

If I faced this identical challenge again I might make the opposite choice. I doubt that I would be consistent.

If the choice had been between opening the window to let in the fresh air or closing it to keep the mosquitoes out, the solution would be simple. Just put in a screen. But in many choices there is no slick technological solution.

· Which is more important, a cool house or a lovely view? The answer determines whether to plant a tree in front of a window.

Those cases come from my own life. By paying attention to the decisions you make from day to day, you will be able to collect your own list. As you make your decisions — for you are compelled by circumstance to decide — you may ask yourself exactly how you decide. I suspect that in the case of a tossup you will find, when you look inside yourself, the inevitable presence of the "gap" or "leap" when, so to speak, reasoning stops and you simply close your eyes and plunge in. It as though when making a difficult decision we momentarily black out, and come up with a resolution, during a brief instant when we execute a remarkable balancing act.

The comparisons become more complicated when they concern government and the public, as the following cases show.

· The judge who decides whether the salary of a public employee must be made public balances the employee's right to privacy with the right of the public to know how its taxes are spent. Different judges, different outcomes.

· That is minor when compared to the many choices Lincoln had to make. As just one example described by Doris Goodwin in *Team of Rivals*, he had to decide "between a surrender [of Fort Sumter] that might compromise the honor of the North and tear it apart, or a reinforcement that might carry the country into civil war." This illustrates how many of the big decisions take the form of a choice between incomparables.

· How do we compare our interests with those of our children and grandchildren? Writing about the limited reserves of petroleum, Daniel Yergin, in his book, *The Prize*, raised that question: "There is that overarching clash, perhaps the one most difficult to figure out. How does one balance "today" against "tomorrow"— the interests of the generation of the 1990s against those who will be living in 2052 and 2092? What is to be given up today for the benefit of future generations?"

We don't worry much about such concerns because we think that science will rescue the future from any mess we leave it.

· In *House of Sand and Fog,* by Andre Dubus III, I found this advice on how to deal with incomparables:

"It's easy. On one side of the page you got your costs and on the other side your benefits. All you do is mark which one is which, then you weigh one side against the other and you get your decision just like that. That's all you ever have to do."

The rub comes in the little phrase "you weigh." That's the heart of the mystery. How do we "weigh?" We cannot put the risks and benefits or the two alternatives on the two pans of a scale and see which pan sinks and which rises.

· In an essay, *Existentialism,* Sartre describes the choice a student of his faced during World War II. The young man could stay home with his mother, who lived alone with him and was suffering from the death of her other son during the German invasion of France, or he could try to join the Free French Forces in England and avenge the death of his brother. This choice was complicated by the risk of being caught before he ever reached England. As Sartre points out, the choice boils down to "Which does more good, the vague act of fighting in a group, or the concrete one of helping a particular human being to go on living? Who can decide *a priori?* Nobody. No book of ethics can tell him."

· Nor can ethics help us choose between safety and learning more about the cosmos. Sean O'Keefe, as head of NASA, had to make that choice, when he cancelled the final repair mission to the Hubbell telescope. "In making my decision I had to balance the world-class science that the Hubbell has produced, and will continue to produce, against the risks to the shuttle and its crew. The safety considerations tipped the scales." The invisible scales could easily have tilted the other way, as evidenced by the decision by O'Keefe's successor, Michael Griffen, to send astronauts to the telescope.

SOCIETY CHOOSES

Choices with this same form, "apples versus oranges," but far more momentous, often confront society. The more controversial they are, the more likely that they involve a comparison of incomparables.

> · The leaders running the Vietnam War faced countless such choices. I mention just one, described by Robert S. McNamara in *In Retrospect*. It concerns whether a pause in our bombing of North Vietnam should be extended:

> *I stressed my judgment that the possibility of sparking talks that might ultimately lead to peace outweighed the military disadvantages of deferring resumption of the bombing pause.*

That choice involved only two incomparables, bombing and not bombing, each with military and psychological consequences. The next one is more complicated.

> · The Congress, unable to agree on how many miles a car should travel on a gallon, ordered the National Highway Traffic and Safety Administration (NHTSA) to set fuel standards. Moreover, it should "consider technological feasibility, economic practicality, the effect of other vehicle standards of the Government on fuel economy, and the need of the United States to conserve energy" On another occasion it was to consider "safety, technology, dependence on foreign oil, and impact on the automobile industry."

We can see why the Congress has trouble resolving the question and passes the buck. NHTSA had to "consider" four incomparable concerns. That word "consider" raises questions that could keep a philosopher busy for a lifetime.

When I imagine being assigned such a task, my mind clouds over. How would I be expected to balance "feasibility" with "economic practicality" or with "the need to conserve energy?"

Even if I could quantify each of the four factors, what could I do with the numbers? What assumptions, what trade-offs would I be able to program for a computer to crunch?

Whatever NHTSA recommends is more credible, less open to criticism, if announced without its supporting rationale. That rationale, necessarily depending on a comparison of incomparables, can seem arbitrary, even biased. No matter how persuasive the reasoning, there will be a point in it where all the data and logic end, the "weighing" of all the pros and cons is done, and the leap to the conclusion occurs. It is a gap that we are so used to that we don't notice it. If we saw such a leap in the midst of a proof of the Theorem of Pythagoras, we would demand, "Exactly how did you get from here to there? A step is missing." We could make the same demand in worldly matters. We don't because, deep down, we recognize that the standards are much looser.

Moreover, by omitting the details of their thinking, the authorities imply that their logic is too complex to be understood by us outsiders. In this way they gain the confidence of the public while making themselves less vulnerable to criticism.

When NHTSA makes its recommendation, there must be a point during its testimony when a Senator could ask, "And exactly how did you decide on this particular solution?" However, no tactful Senator would want to call attention to the inevitable gap that logic cannot cross. What mysterious process is hidden in that word, "decide"?

Mathematics sheds no light on the resolution. It offers no escape from the problem. It can find the shape of the quart can that uses the least metal, but it can't meet Congress's request. In cost-benefit analysis each factor is allegedly given a monetary value, so the problem reduces to a comparison of two numbers, the cost and the benefit. As in a business, there then is a bottom line. However, if the details of the computations are revealed, the analysis is vulnerable to criticism and may lose its credibility.

THE WHOLE PRODUCE SECTION

This archetypal choice, which involves several incomparables, like apples, oranges, and bananas, or even a whole produce section, is typical of the challenge a person or a society faces when trying to reconcile incomparable values.

· In an article titled *Dams in Distress*, Frederic Schwarz

described the problems that pop up when deciding whether to demolish a dam: "The question of dam removal is an important one, taking in issues of habitat conservation, changes in industry, the ownership of natural resources, Indian rights, the claims of local residents against those of the larger community, and even the very notion of progress." Pause a moment to consider how you would go about reaching a decision. Then imagine trying to defend that decision in a room where all the factions are represented.

· Bruce Babbitt, when he was Secretary of the Interior, had to deal with such challenges: "There's a huge collection of academic literature on all this, and I've found it fairly unsatisfactory. It all comes down to quantifying economic activity, and I don't know if you can do that on any piece of landscape. We know the cost of everything and the value of nothing, is what this is all about. You can't just cost this stuff out." Which leaves us with the question, "What do you do?"

What would you or I do if we had to implement the Federal Land Policy and Management Act of 1976, where we read that the Secretary,

In the development of land use plans shall observe the principles of multiple use; use a systematic interdisciplinary approach to achieve integrated consideration of physical, biological, economic, and other sciences; give priority to areas of critical environmental concern; consider present and potential uses of the public lands; consider the relative scarcity of the values involved and the availability of alternative means; weigh long-term benefits to the public against short-term benefits; comply with pollution control laws

Not a simple assignment.

· The down-to-earth California highway code orders officials to consider even more factors: "Community values; recreational, aesthetic, and park values, historical value and impact on local tax rolls and local traffic." But, as is to be expected, the code offers no guidance on just how these diverse concerns are to be balanced. This omission may be inevitable. What we think of as "rational" can go only so far when we must choose between incomparables. That tends to make choice unpredictable, which adds to the murkiness of the future.

Given the variety of concerns in our society, we can expect such disparate values to bump into each other often. Moreover, as the population grows and the land is built up, such conflicts will become more frequent.

· The Chairman of the Council on Environmental Quality, James Connaughton, made the resolution of such conflicts sound simple. "Our approach is to maximize the quality of life in America. That means balancing the environmental equation with the natural resource equation, the social equation, and the economic equation." But there are no "equations" in the mathematical sense, though the term does lend a tone of deep analysis to the deliberation. Reconciling the various qualities, some of which elude the grasp of numbers, may depend less on complex reasoning than on the agenda of whoever happens to be in charge at the moment.

· Perhaps the ultimate attempts to deal with a host of incomparables are the Copenhagen Conferences of 2004 and 2008. Lomborg, who we met in Chapter 3, invited eight leading economists, including Nobel Prize winners, to decide how best to allocate a theoretical amount of money to address some of the problems facing the world. They had to compare such options as solving global warming, immunizing children, liberalizing trade, controlling AIDS, and reducing malaria. Not an easy task. More interesting than how they would spend the money would be the details of how they reached their decision.

THE PLAN AND THE PLANET

A scenario that pits a new project against the preservation of nature is so frequent that it should have a name, maybe "The plan versus the planet." There is usually no midway point to serve as a compromise. It's either undertake the project or not.

The confrontation of man and nature arose early in the twentieth century in the debate about damming the Hetch-Hetchy valley to provide water for San Francisco. Gifford Pinchot and John Muir, both environmentalists, expressed the choice in its archetypal simplicity. Pinchot argued, "I am fully persuaded the injury caused by substituting a lake for the present swampy floor of the Hetch Hetchy Valley is altogether unimportant compared with the benefits to be derived from its use as a reservoir." Muir had quite a different perspective: "Dam Hetch Hetchy? As well dam for water tanks the people's cathedrals and churches, for no holier temple has ever been consecrated by the heart of man." The valley was dammed.

The way in which the arguments and values in choices like this one are weighed against each other merits scrutiny. Up to a certain moment a person compares, weighs, balances; then somehow, by some means, manages to make a choice. Exactly what happens at that moment, how a person manages to avoid perpetual indecision but comes down on one side or the other, is a mystery that deserves to be plumbed.

In *Judgement and Choice* R. Hogarth, recognized this challenge:

> *People are generally unaware of how they make decisions and often why they prefer one alternative to others. They show little concern for the quality of their own decision-making processes (although the failures of others are often indicated with haste). The scientific study of decision making has not attracted the attention it merits.*

Psychologists could carry out in-depth interviews of those who have just chosen between incomparables in the real world. Exactly how did they "take everything into consideration" or "balance pros and cons"? What are the imponderables that lie deep in the unconscious, the half-forgotten memories, or the fleeting passions of the moment, that determine the decisions? In another approach, neuroscientists believe that they have found the small part of the brain that seems to be dedicated to resolving the choice between incomparables. If so, how does that small part make the choice?

Of course, if we concentrate on how we compare incomparables, we may never be able to reach a decision. Like the tightrope performer, it is best to look straight ahead, not down at the details of what we are doing.

Until the neurologists, psychologists, and decision theorists figure out how we manage to decide, we will muddle along. In the meantime we can look within ourselves as we make those common apples-versus-oranges decisions. We may discover and admit that there is a limit to the role of reason. In desperation we may give up and call in someone we view as wise to decide for us. But then we must ask, "How do we know that someone is any wiser than we are?" I don't know the answer, but I return to this important question in the chapters devoted to the two roles of the "expert."

9 Hidden Choice

Implicit choice; Troublemakers;
Varieties of implicit chooice; Abandon luxuries.

When we look within ourselves we may wonder how we manage to choose between incomparables, and not just struggle forever to make up our minds. However, another type of choice may be more common, yet we don't even know at the time we face it that we are making a choice. In this case, we don't notice the alternatives to those we focus on. By a quirk, they lack an advocate. They are mute and invisible. This type of choice I call "implicit" or "hidden." In a hidden choice, we choose, but we do so unaware of the rejected options, which no one mentioned.

IMPLICIT CHOICE

The alternatives are just as real as the alternatives conspicuous in the sunlight. Sometimes, long after our conscious choosing is over, circumstance lifts the alternatives out of their obscurity.

I will offer enough examples to show that the hidden choice is common. Moreover it can be just as significant as our explicit choices.

> · Over 1.3 million viewers paid $50 each to watch a boxing match on TV. That adds up to 65 million discretionary dollars. Every year Americans spend over 30 billion dollars on weight-loss programs and diet products. The yearly

cost of bubble gum, candy, or pet food is measured in the billions of dollars. Personal tanning runs up a 5-billion-dollar annual bill.

A billion dollars may not seem like much anymore. It's less than a four-dollar contribution from every American. Or it's about 32,000 workers, each earning $32,000. Still, it's not trivial.

Every time we spend a dollar for something we are, obviously, not spending it on something else. When we buy a package of bubble gum we are not thinking about, say, saving a wetland in Florida. Whether or not we are aware of this, we are nevertheless making an implicit choice, bubble gum over wetland. We are fortunate that we manage to avoid the countless real choices between incomparables that lurk silently in the background. If we had to deal consciously with every one of those silent alternatives we might never decide anything. Like Hamlet, we would be unable to act

TROUBLEMAKERS

Unfortunately for our peace of mind, troublemakers, who want to influence our choices, transform the implicit into the explicit. They lift the covert alternatives out of their natural habitat and dangle them before our eyes. Then we can no longer pretend that they aren't there. It isn't often that we are so blatantly confronted, but when we are trapped by such a ruse our choices instantly become more complicated.

I will cite a few cases where someone becomes a spokesperson for an implicit option. It is easy to extend the list. Indeed, the implicit choice may be more common than the explicit choice. The implicit choices may have more impact on our way of life and on the world of our children and grandchildren than the choices that dominate our public debates.

· Christina Morin at age seventeen on a family safari spent four days with the impoverished Samburu tribe in Africa. Returning home, she raised thousands of dollars to help them survive. "I take the money I'd spend on CDs or a soda and throw it in a jar for the Samburu."

Before the safari, Christina was making an implicit choice: buy a CD or help the Samburu. She had never heard of the Samburu or their plight. The trip made the implicit choice explicit. Publicity for her campaign made that type of choice explicit for thousands of people. That doesn't mean that they will all throw money into a jar. It does mean that those who don't are making an explicit choice not to. The alternatives found a voice. People who hear that voice are forced to decide whether to contribute to help the Samburu.

· The military establishment spends a good fraction of the national budget. As a result it provides an often-used source of hidden choices made explicit. Whether to show that some civilian program is a bargain or to show that some new weapon system is an extravagance, such choices, though rhetorical, are so frequent that they have earned a name, "guns versus butter."

· A critic of military boondoggles noted that the budget for Armed Forces recruiting would pay for the entire educational system of three cities the size of Washington, D.C. Or to put it another way, it would provide 60,000 full four-year college scholarships. Though he had exposed an implicit choice, he did not try to replace recruitment with scholarships.

· John Friedman applied this technique to the war in Iraq:

Each day an estimated $195 million is being spent — money that could provide twelve meals to every starving child in the world . . . In addition, one day of Iraq War expenses could cover what the College Board estimates to be the full cost of a public higher education for some 17,000 American students.

· An advocate for two redwood parks instead of one, pointed out that "We are not buying a wife. There is nothing immoral about two redwood parks. And the cost? It might cost $100 million to buy both watersheds. Perhaps you are thinking that it is a wad of dough. Maybe it is. It's five supersonic jet transports. It's four days of war."

· The website *National Priorities* has pursued the hidden choice to its limits. There you can click on your state or even congressional district and also on some expensive program and discover what could be accomplished if the program were scrapped and its funds diverted to a civilian project.

· Whether a guns-versus-butter choice is fictitious has long been a subject of dispute. This exchange is typical: An opponent of a proposed antiballistic missile system wrote,

The failure to spend $800 million on relieving the underprivileged poor and oppressed — and spending such funds instead on the ABM system — would indeed be gambling with the lives of untold Americans for several generations. The moral decision in a choice between these two alternatives is clear. Our resources must be spent to raise the level of living of untold millions, who would be the greatest source of security for this nation.

A rebuttal challenged the reality of the choice, *"It poses a false dilemma. The American people will never be confronted with a clear decision to spend $10 billion either for an ABM system or for domestic programs. Our system does not operate that way. Recent history provides little or no evidence that 'savings' from defense cuts have been transferred to any other program. Each 'cause' has to compete on its own merits in the political marketplace."*

If our resources were unbounded, then the dilemma would indeed be contrived; the implicit choice would be fictitious. But in a finite budget the items do compete with each other. That is the view of two of our Presidents.

· When President Eisenhower was told by the military that a Vietnam war would cost at least $3.5 billion a year, he asked his Secretary of Treasury, "What would that do to the budget?" "It would mean a deficit, Mr. President," he replied, and with that any chance of immediate intervention vanished.

· A decade later President Johnson concealed the cost of our involvement in Vietnam, for, "If I talk about the cost of the war, the Great Society won't go through. Old Wilbur Mills will send me back the Great Society and then he'll tell me they'll be glad to spend whatever we need for the war."

Both saw their choices as real. At another time Eisenhower left no doubt about his belief: "Every gun that is made, every warship launched, every rocket, signifies a theft from those who hunger and are not fed, those who are cold and are not clothed." Even so, though faced explicitly, the choice remains remote and intangible. We do not snatch the food from the hungry and sell it to pay for the guns. We do not cancel an order for guns and divert the savings to feed the hungry. Still, to claim that the choice is fictitious is to pretend that we live in an era of infinite resources. As the resources and budget get tighter, the implicit choice of guns versus butter will become more frequently explicit and controversial.

THE VARIETIES OF IMPLICIT CHOICE

· An opponent of a $49 raise in taxes for parks in Davis, California used the hidden-choice gambit:

I can think of dozens of ways to spend $49. Give it to the American Cancer Society. Provide piano lessons for a student who can't afford them. Support a park in a city that has no parks at all.

The bond was defeated, but there is no sign that the $49 saved went to these good causes.

· Katha Pollitt, bemoaning the amount spent on Christmas presents that will languish on a closet floor, listed several causes, with their addresses, where dollars could be better spent: a woman's school in Afghanistan, a library in a poor school in New York City, or high school tuition for a qualified student in Africa. I wonder how many donations her request inspired.

· Those examples concern the implicit choice in the way we spend money. But there is also the implicit choice in how we spend time, as Stanton Price wrote to the New York Times on February 1, 2004, in response to Michael Jackson's fans' support of him during his legal problems: "Many of those fans ... will find they can't get a decent job, more pay in the job they have, affordable housing, health insurance ...And they will never know that at least some of this could have been avoided if they had devoted their time and energy to Sacramento and Washington rather than to Michael Jackson."

That letter appeared on Super Bowl Sunday. Another letter could have made the same point, that time spent watching a football go back and forth could have been better spent in an election year. More realistically, perhaps we should all tithe our time to democracy: For every ten hours we spend being entertained at sports events or concerts, we spend an hour digging deeper behind the issues of the day, even reading background books.

Rocky Anderson, when mayor of Salt Lake City, raised the same point more dramatically in an address October 27, 2007:

> How many people can honestly say they have spent as much time learning about and opposing the outrages of the . . . administration as they have spent watching sports or mindless television programs . . ? Escapist, time-sapping sports and insipid entertainment have indeed become the opiate of the masses. Why is this country so sound asleep? Why do we abide what is happening to our nation, to our Constitution, to the cause of peace and international law and order? . . . How much will you put up with before you say "No more" and mean it?

Though he was thinking only about the administration of the moment, his words send a timeless message: a well-functioning democracy depends on an informed and active people. When we choose to abdicate, others, perhaps with suspect motives, will fill the gap.

We become the choices we make, whether we make them consciously or unconsciously. Both types have the same impact on the world.

ABANDON LUXURIES?

My final example is no rhetorical gambit. It treats the invisible hidden choice quite seriously, insisting that it is as real as any explicit choice.

The moral philosopher, Peter Singer, found that a $200 donation would help a sickly two-year-old child become a healthy six-year-old and offer safe passage through childhood's most perilous years. He advised, "You shouldn't buy that new car, take that cruise, redecorate the house, or get that pricey new suit." After all, $1000 could save the lives of five children.

He goes on, "Whatever money you're spending on luxuries, not necessities, should be given away."

For emphasis he reminds us,

> *If we value the life of a child more than going to fancy restaurants, the next time we dine out we will know that we could have done something better with our money.*

If that is not enough to persuade us to share our wealth, then he leaves no room for ambiguity.

> *If we don't do it, then we should at least know we are failing to live a morally decent life -- not because it is good to wallow in guilt but because knowing where we should be going is the first step toward heading in the right direction.*

In an article titled "What Should a Billionaire Give — and What Should You" he even suggests how much we should donate.

We can't escape by asking him whether he practices what he preaches. I hear that he does.

Try as I may, I have not been able to punch a hole in Singer's logic. I suppose if I visited the underdeveloped world, its poverty would become real. Like Christina Morin, I would be moved to obey the professor's command. Or, if his message were repeated by every priest, minister, rabbi, mullah, news anchor, and talk show host, even by the President, I could not evade it. Now I can label Singer an idealist. But deep down I know he is the realist, that what he says is right. He resembles the ancient prophets who scolded the people for their evil ways. Like the prophets, he has, so far as I know, had little effect. The implicit choice has become explicit, but I try to suppress it, though his argument has at least both made me more generous and also increased my sense of guilt when I indulge in some luxury.

Just as "guns versus butter" is a special type of implicit choice, implicit choice, in turn, is usually a special case of "apples versus oranges." What makes it special is that the alternatives are not listed on the screen.

NUMBER

10 Beware the Number

The charm of numbers; A pollster interviews me;
Practice Skepticism.

A number, however erroneous, is more convincing than a word, however apt. We occupants of the outer ring must stay on the alert, ready to question any number. We should be ready to speak up: "Where did that number come from?" "Show me the raw data." "What assumptions did you feed into the computer?" "May I see the calculations?" That way we can strip numbers of their magic spell and level the playing field.

Numbers suggest the disciplined analysis of science. Numbers that have passed through the black box of a computer exert even more power. "Zero-defect" design, a term spun off from space technology, carries more weight than "flawless." "Zero population growth" seems to say more than "static population." Whoever uses zero appears to be well trained in science and comfortable with mathematics, qualities useful for intimidating most of us laypersons.

Because of my job I am comfortable with numbers. They are my friends. I even have favorites among them, such as three-fifths, a pleasant fraction, which I feel is neglected. But many people find numbers frightening.

When I first began looking at how decisions are made in the real world, I had hopes that by exploiting numbers more, we could settle issues at least a bit more calmly and wisely. However, as I saw how they are used I lost hope that they would help.

THE CHARM OF NUMBERS

Numbers, like words, can have emotional connotations, which may affect us when they appear in a polemic. Skyscrapers often lack a floor numbered 13. The Jet Blue terminal at the Kennedy airport lacks a gate number 13, though it has gates numbered 12 and 14. The composer Arnold Schoenberg was so scared of the number 13 that later in life he numbered his measures 12, 12A, 14, skipping the dreaded number. He explained that, "It's not a superstition, it is belief." He expected he would die on the 13th of a month in his 76th year, 7 + 6 being 13, and he did.

Woodrow Wilson also gave 13 magic powers, but for him they were auspicious. In 1919, the first draft of his League of Nations was ready on February 13th and consisted of 26 (twice 13) articles. These he saw as signs that his League would succeed. By 1920, when the United States failed to join it, it was doomed. So much for the magic of 13. Wilson should have checked with Schoenberg.

Some people avoid living in a house with the address 666, viewed as the sign of the devil. But a string of 0's pleases: we watch in suspense as the odometer in the dashboard slowly replaces a string of 9's with 0's.

To appreciate the magic of numbers ending in 0's, go back to the last day of the 1941 baseball season. Before the game started, Ted Williams was batting .39955, which rounds up to a beautiful .400. But Williams, unwilling to settle for a fraudulent .400 with an asterisk, insisted on playing, and ended up with .406, becoming the last player to reach the mythical .400.

But numbers work their charm not only when creating sports heroes. They play a role in shaping major decisions.

WHERE DID IT COME FROM?

When a number enters a debate it is often a conversation stopper. We ordinary mortals assume that some specialist employing deep reasoning, sophisticated mathematics, and objective raw data, perhaps crunching all this in a computer that executes a billion operations per second, has come up with the number. We, in awe, may be reluctant to ask, "How did you find that number? What were your assumptions?" We should not accept as an answer, "I don't know. Our consultant did it," or "The computer did it."

Once a number flows into the media stream, it takes on a life of its own. Like a rumor, its origin gets lost. It is as hard to remove it as it is to extract the yolk from scrambled eggs.

· Officials have claimed that we intercept only ten percent of the drugs entering this country. Where did that figure come from? If you stop to think about it, you may well wonder how anyone could ever calculate it. How do you estimate the part never seen?

It turns out, according to a government official, who chooses to remain anonymous, that, "There is no way of telling. It's a matter of your best guess." "Ten percent" was produced by a law enforcement official pressed for a precise number at a Congressional hearing. A police officer once characterized such numbers as "pulled from the air." They are so common they even go by an acronym, PFA.

· In 1983, the Department of Health and Human Services reckoned that 1.5 million children are reported missing each year. That led to a campaign advising children how not to be kidnapped, and distributing pictures of missing children on milk cartons.

Later studies showed that fewer than 5000 children were abducted by strangers but that over 350,000 children are snatched by parents during custody disputes. The total was far less than the original 1.5 million. The media's focus on a few spectacular kidnappings by strangers dominated the layperson's perception.

· In July, 2005, Fortune magazine frightened its readers with the news that a year before, China produced 600,000 engineers and the United States a mere 70,000. The National Academy of Sciences, in a 543-page report titled "Rising Above the Gathering Storm," cited those alarming statistics. The numbers traveled to the New York Times, the Boston Globe, and the web. Where did they come from? Carl Bialik, the "Numbers Guy" in the Wall Street Journal, was suspicious, and decided to find out.

He discovered that the word "engineers" in Chinese includes people who in the United States would be called "technicians." Moreover, many of these "engineers" would not meet American standards. In December, 2005, Duke University concluded that the United States produces about 140,000 engineers, more per capita than China, which produces about 350,000. However, that figure of 600,000 was still quoted in 2006 by Senator John Warner at a science exposition for middle-school children.

A POLLSTER INTERVIEWS ME

Numbers coming from polls should be viewed with suspicion, as I found out first hand. I was once called up by a pollster, who wanted to learn which cities I thought were dangerous and which safe. Our conversation went something like this.

Pollster: *"New York?"*

Stein: *"It all depends. If you stay out of certain areas, especially Central Park at night, it's pretty safe."*

Pollster: *"Would you say it's 'safe' or 'dangerous'?"*

Stein: *"Safe," I replied, feeling that New York could use some favorable publicity.*

Pollster: *"Los Angeles?"*

Stein: *"Dangerous," for that would make New York look even better.*

Pollster: *"Chicago?"*

Stein: *"Safe." Though I had no idea, I knew that it had broken up Al Capone's gang long ago.*

Pollster: *"Minneapolis?"*

Stein: *"Safe," for I was loyal to the city of my birth.*

This went on through many cities. I answered, in part to cheer the interviewer who might have had to meet a quota.

My experience may be typical. Most of us dwell in the outer ring and lack solid information about practically everything. That our responses to polls are so sensitive to their wording shows how thin is the veneer of our knowledge.

We are inundated with numbers. "Fifty percent of marriages begun this year will end in divorce." "Inflation is running at two percent." "The expected life span of a male born today is 71 years." If we imagine ourselves or anyone else calculating these numbers, some of which involve predictions far into the future, we realize that they will involve guesses, questionable data, and debatable assumptions. We would not be surprised if two statisticians, working independently, arrived at different numbers.

PRACTICE SKEPTICISM

Imagine that someone tells you to calculate the rate of inflation. First there is the matter of its definition. Just how would you define it? Second, it involves comparing price levels a year apart. How do you compute a price level? If these price levels are reliable to only two significant digits, then a change, from 326 to 328, say, would be meaningless. The inflation rate would seem to be 2/326 or about one percent. However, the 2 in the numerator is meaningless. So one is dividing a meaningless number by 326.

Yet the nation needs something called "the rate of inflation," which is mentioned in pension plans and labor contracts. I do not envy the econometricians who must deal with such a slippery number.

It is quite common for an error of at least two percent to occur in measuring economic data. Oskar Morgenstern, in *On the Accuracy of Economic Data*, discussed this in the case of the gross national product: "A reliable growth rate of two significant digits is impossible to establish. But even the first digit is in grave doubt. Yet the public discussion is on the second digit, usually the first decimal, and it is carried on in all seriousness as if a distinction between, say, 3.2 and 3.3 percent were really possible." Even so, the stock market fluctuates by billions of dollars in response to such numbers.

It is the statistician's business to quantify the sources of uncertainty and present them along with the analysis. The estimate of possible error is usually presented in the report of an opinion poll. Knowing that there is an error of any kind nourishes a healthy skepticism.

Bishop Berkeley in 1734 spoke up for those of us high up in the bleachers when he addressed the mathematicians of his time in his book *The Analyst*, "You, gentlemen, who are presumed to be of all men the greatest masters of reason. It is supposed that you apprehend more distinctly, consider more closely, infer more justly, conclude more accurately than other men." Even now the argument couched in numbers is more convincing than mere words. A number is precise and fixed. A word is vague. Its meaning changes with events. "Appeasement" meant one thing before Munich, and another after. "Five" or "two-thirds" mean the same today as a millennium ago or as they will a millennium from now.

This report from the chief of the pacification program in the Vietnam War deftly exploited the magical power of numbers: "Two thirds of the people now live in secure areas. The computerized Hamlet-Evacuation System provides a detailed monthly check on the allegiance of those living in the 12,600 cities and hamlets. The secure population has increased more than a million since last January."

The numbers, such as 2/3, 12,600, and a million, announce that "no fuzzy thinkers are here." The superfluous adjective "computerized" further awes any potential critic.

In any case, when we see a number used in the midst of a contentious issue, we should demand to see where it came from. The task may be harder than finding the source of the Nile.

For practice, you could try to discover the origin of the advice to drink at least eight glasses of water a day. My own attempt failed.

This chapter is a warning not to let fuzzy thinking hide in precise numbers. I am not saying that numbers should be avoided. Later, in discussing prediction, which is a key part of choice, I even urge that numbers can play a bigger role than they do now.

11 Second Warning about Numbers

*Length and weight are easy; Consistency;
Inconsistent dice*

Much to my disappointment, not everything can be put on a scale and measured. We are tempted to believe that anything named by a single word can be measured by a single number. For instance, "intelligence," whatever that is, we pretend to measure by a number, the IQ, or intelligence quotient.

Yet we must be cautious when we try to impose a number where it doesn't belong. The burden of proof that a number can measure some quality rests upon those who claim that a scale can be found. To see why there may be trouble, first take a close look at some qualities we can easily measure, for instance, "length" and "weight."

LENGTH AND WEIGHT ARE EASY

Before we could ever measure "length" we already had the notion of "longer than." To decide which of two sticks is longer, we could line them up next to each other. There was no need to refer to numbers. We knew that if stick A is longer than stick B, and if stick B is longer than stick C, then stick A is longer than stick C. Call this property of sticks "consistency."

If lengths can be measured by numbers, then sticks must be consistent, because numbers are. That is, if number a is bigger than number b, and number b is bigger than number c, then a is bigger than c. For instance, 6 is bigger than 5, and 5 is bigger than 4, and, no surprise, 6 is indeed bigger than 4.

We measure lengths by selecting one stick to serve as the unit, calling its length "1." By laying off this stick along any other stick, we get numbers to measure lengths.

Similarly, the notion "heavier than" can be defined without recourse to a measure of "heaviness." To decide which of two objects is heavier, put them on two pans of a balance and see which pan goes down. Simple experiments show that if rock A is heavier than rock B, and rock B is heavier than rock C, then rock A is heavier than rock C. Because "heavier than" is consistent, there is hope that "heaviness" can be measured by numbers. And it is, as anyone knows who has stepped on a scale.

Comparisons, such as "longer than," "heavier than," and "hotter than," must be consistent if they are ever to be reduced to deciding which of two numbers is larger. The presence of even a single inconsistency would prevent the introduction of a numerical scale.

CONSISTENCY

Our belief that comparisons are consistent begins early, when we start to use words like "longer" and "better." Subconsciously we may picture the objects judged as lining up in single file from longest to shortest or from best to worst. Such an arrangement suggests a value by which we make our judgments, and behind it, a numerical scale.

Inconsistency represents the conflict between the simplicity we expect and the complexity of the world in which we live. However, inconsistency can thrive in the midst of our most reasonable ways of reaching a decision.

Imagine that there are three candidates for a secretarial position: Arthur, Bob, and Charles. In *experience*, Arthur is first, Bob is second, and Charles is third. In *typing speed*, Bob is first, Charles second, and Arthur third. In *dependability* Charles is first, Arthur second, and Bob third,

Since Arthur outranks Bob on two factors, experience and dependability, Arthur is preferable to Bob. Similarly, Bob is preferable to Charles, outranking him in experience and typing. For consistency to hold, Arthur should outrank Charles, but a quick check shows that Charles outranks Arthur.

The inconsistency arises from an attempt to combine several scales into one, which can then be used to decide who is "best." In spite of this, the company does manage to hire of one of them.

Even at a personal level we can experience an inconsistency. Say that we are comparing an orange, an apple, and a banana. We may prefer the orange to the apple because it's juicier, and the apple to the banana because it's crisper. Even so we may prefer the banana to the orange because of its flavor.

We should expect that there is no way to measure "intelligence" because it is difficult if not impossible to decide which of two people is "smarter" or "more intelligent." One of them, for instance, may be more gifted in music, Mozart, for instance, and the other, more adept in science, Einstein, for instance.

The seeming paradox of inconsistency is simply the conflict between the "real world" and our model. On first seeing it, we assume that it is reality that misbehaves. But the culprit is the model in our mind, with its naive notion of consistency.

THE INCONSISTENT DICE

Inconsistency shows up even in things so tangible that we can make them out of wood. The figure on the next page shows three dice. They are *not* the usual ones, with their six faces displaying from one to six dots. One has four faces with five dots and two faces with one dot. On another all the faces have four dots. The third has four faces with two dots and two faces with six dots. Call them A, B, and C, as shown on the next page.

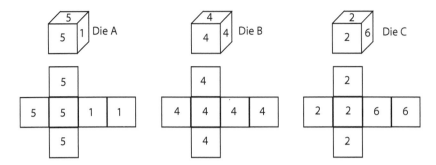

Each of two players picks one of the three dice. In a game the players roll the dice, and the one with the higher number on top wins. The players keep their chosen dice and play many times. Which of the three dice is the best one to play with?

Let's compare die A with die B. Die A will win whenever it comes up 5. Otherwise, it will lose. So it will tend to win in about 4 out of 6 times in the long run. Die B, then, will tend to win in about 2 out of 6 times. That tells us die A is better than die B.

Next compare die B with die C. Die B will win whenever die C shows a 2, which is about 4 out of 6 times in the long run. So die B is better than die C.

Intuition then tells us that die A should be better than die C. Well, it isn't. A bit longer calculation shows that die C defeats die A 5 out of 9 times, which is more than one-half, in the long run. We have yet another example of inconsistency. This one was invented by the statistician Bradley Efron. [To see why C defeats A 5 out of 9 times, note first that in a third of the tosses C will show a 6 and win no matter what A does. But C also beats A if C comes up with a 2 and A has only a 1. The 2 shows up two-thirds of the times, and in a third of those times, A has a 1. So two-ninths of the times, C defeats A this way. The sum of 1/3 and 2/9 is 5/9.]

In practical terms it means that whichever die you choose, your opponent can choose a better one. That implies it is better to choose after your opponent has chosen. There is no "best" die. There is no way to devise a numerical scale of dice so that the one with the larger number on the scale tends to win against the one with the smaller number.

This suggests taking three of Efron's dice to Las Vegas and, being courteous, offering your opponent first choice. No matter what that choice is, you will be able to choose a die that will beat it in the long run.

Inconsistency is like Escher's optical illusion of a staircase that rises with each step yet, after many steps and turns, reaches its starting level. But, unlike an Escher fantasy, inconsistency can be quite real. We may find the inconsistency of the dice counter-intuitive, but the dice are happy.

Mass, length and time, the three basic concepts of elementary physics, can be measured to many decimal places. But the concepts that often occur in decisions may elude the grasp of numbers. Inconsistency is just one of the reasons. We seldom can call upon numbers to help us escape the need to compare incomparables. Those who try, no matter how cleverly, will find themselves reinventing the flat tire.

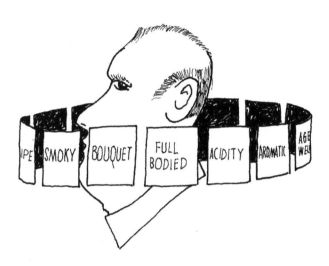

12 Third Warning about Numbers

One number won't do; One word,
but not one number.

There's another reason why numbers will not save us from having to make choices by means we don't understand. It's that our values are so complex, they are not like vegetables in a grocery, where everything has a price tag.

I'll begin by describing a quality that can be measured by a single number and then a slight variation that cannot. This example uses nothing more than rectangles and triangles, but it illustrates the problem of trying to measure even a simple quality.

ONE NUMBER WON'T DO

Can the "shape" of a rectangle be measured by a single number? Two rectangles of different sizes may have the same shape. These two are the same shape, their length being twice their width:

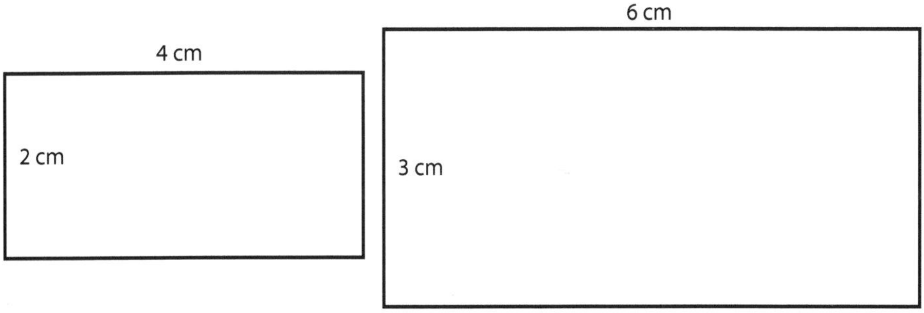

4 cm

2 cm

6 cm

3 cm

All squares have the same shape. In each one the length equals the width. In other words, the ratio of length to width is one. This suggests a way of measuring the shape of a rectangle by a single number: just divide its length by its width. Since the length is always at least as large as the width, the "shape number" of a rectangle is at least 1. Every square has a shape number 1.

The rectangles in the diagram have a shape number of 2. A rectangle whose length is much greater than its width has a very large shape number.

So there is a scale for the shapes of rectangles, just as there is for weights or lengths.

Can we record the shape of a triangle with only a single number, as we did with rectangles? The two triangles in the top half of the figure below have the same shape. They look alike except for their size. One is just a blowup of the other.

The three triangles in the lower half of the figure all have different shapes. They should have different "shape numbers."

Can we measure all possible triangular shapes on a single scale, as we can with rectangles? I will show that this is impossible.

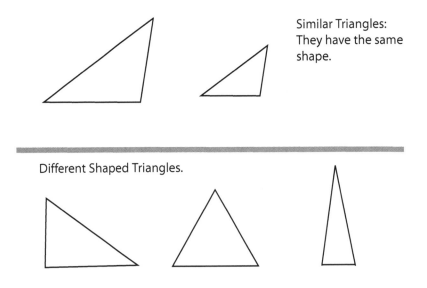

Similar Triangles: They have the same shape.

Different Shaped Triangles.

When do two triangles have the same shape? Only if the three angles in one of them are the same as the three angles in the other. For instance, all triangles with angles 40°, 60°, and 80° have the same shape.

In short, the three angles in a triangle determine its shape. It seems that we need three numbers. However, we can get by with just two. Since the three angles must add up to 180°, if we know two of them we can figure out the third. If two are 40° and 60°, the third must be 80°.

It takes two numbers, not just one, to describe the shape of a triangle. Just specify, say, its two smaller angles. The shape of a triangle is far more complicated than the shape of a rectangle. Unlike lengths or weights, shapes of triangles cannot be put on a number scale. Instead, we need two numbers. Mathematicians say that the space of triangular shapes is "two-dimensional, not one-dimensional."

Instead of shapes, let us take a look at something more complicated: the range of possible colors, which is important to paint and dye manufacturers, color printers, and artists.

Can a color be described by a single number? In other words, can all the colors be arranged along a line? Thinking of the rainbow, which displays red, orange, yellow, green, blue, indigo, violet, and intermediate hues on a line, we may be tempted to say "yes," but the answer is "no."

When you go into a paint store to select a color, you will find pages of color chips arranged not on a line but like the squares in a checkerboard. The colors fill out a page, not just the border of the page. The rainbow appears as part of the border.

Artists know this. One of their first exercises is to make a color wheel. First they put colors around the circumference, using the primary colors — red, blue, and yellow. Then they take two of the colors, such as red and yellow, in all possible proportions, filling in the stretch from red to yellow. This part of the border will go from red, through orange, gradually to yellow. Then they fill in the whole wheel by combining the three primaries in various proportions. Since the three proportions add up to 100%, the proportions of red and blue, say, determine the proportion of yellow. The colors, like the shapes of triangles, form a two-dimensional space.

But artists deal with a space that has an even higher dimension. They must also consider how dark or light a given color may be. This quality, called "value," is recorded in a black and white photograph of a painting. This brings us up to three dimensions. But, in addition, artists must pay attention to luminosity and transparency. It isn't easy, for with these we are up to at least a five-dimensional space. Painting makes the mathematics we meet in school look simple.

As triangular shapes or colors show, some qualities cannot be measured by a single number, cannot be arrayed along a scale. But these examples are much less complex than, say, wine flavors, which are influenced by at least five hundred chemicals. That is why experienced judges, when trying to rank wines at a state fair from best to worst, often disagree with each other and, on retasting, disagree even with themselves.

The conductor who wishes to seat violinists in order of "ability" faces a multidimensional task. A violinist's ability, because it involves interpretation, sight-reading, intonation, tone, and dexterity, is not easy to judge. The choirmaster who arranges singers by height has no such problem since height is a one-dimensional concept.

ONE WORD BUT NOT ONE NUMBER

Even though a quality, such as shape, flavor, color, or intelligence, is named by a single word, it may not be one-dimensional. The range of human "intelligence" is at least as complex as the range of wine flavors. It is preposterous to pretend to reduce it to a single number. After many years' study, the psychologist J. P. Guilford concluded "We may say that there are at least fifty ways of being intelligent ... Simplicity certainly has its appeal. But human nature is exceedingly complex and we may as well face the fact."

The first obstacle to measuring by a single number is inconsistency, described in the preceding chapter. Now we have a second: that a quality — the shapes of triangles, the possible colors — fills out a space more complex than the one-dimensional line. We should not expect the deeper human concerns, like beauty and justice, to fit the mold of a single number, such as its worth in dollars.

The tell-tale sign that some value is not measurable is that it is controversial. Comparisons made in terms of that value trigger endless disputes about the choices that society faces. There may be no "best"way to educate our children nor a "best" way to provide health care. On the other hand, a value we can measure is usually non-controversial.

In any case, there are limits to the use of numbers. We cannot resort to numbers to avoid facing the choice between incomparables. We are left pretending to "weigh" complex values against each other by placing them on the pans of an imaginary balance.

13 Where Did that Number Come from?

*A number for confidence; A number for
the future; What about the CPI?*

The headline reads, "Consumer Confidence Declines for fourth Consecutive Month." It turns out to have fallen from 94.5 in August to 93.3 in September. An alarmed economic advisor lamented, "This was not a report that said consumers were ready to spend, spend, spend."

Let's take a look at the source of such numbers. I warn you that at one point there will be an equation with letters in it. You may skip over that bit. I know that in America it's customary and acceptable, even a sign of a well-balanced personality, not to like mathematics.

A NUMBER FOR CONFIDENCE

For years, I had seen that kind of headline when the Conference Board, a non-governmental group of economists in New York, brought out its monthly estimate of consumer confidence. "Consumers" is the new name for human beings. Out of curiosity, I decided to find out what lies behind the number that presumably reveals how willing people will be to part with their money a few months down the road. No wonder the signal is watched.

Even a slight change in this index spreads joy or grief in the financial community. A change from 94.5 to 93.3, which is barely more than about one part in a hundred, elicits serious pronouncements from pundits. That suggests that Consumer Confidence is measured with remarkably fine calipers.

When I called up the Conference Board, they referred me to their website, but that didn't give me what I wanted. They then sent me their Business Cycle Indicators Handbook, which describes their methods.

Each month they send out 5000 questionnaires to a nationwide sample of households. This sample is freshly chosen every month. About 3500 of the households respond. The index is based on responses concerning five topics:

· Appraisal of current business conditions.

· Expectations for business conditions in six months.

· Appraisal of current employment conditions.

· Expectations for employment six months hence.

· Expectations for family income six months hence

Each question has three possible answers: positive, negative, and neutral.

The Board then massages the numbers with a little arithmetic. For each question, the number of positive responses is divided by the number of positive and negative responses. This proportion is called "the relative value." It is not affected by the number of neutral responses. This relative value is then divided by the relative value for the same question found in the survey of the year 1985, which serves as a benchmark. Finally, that quotient is adjusted for seasonal influences.

The Board then averages the five numbers, one for each question. The Consumer Confidence Index is that average.

I was now much closer to finding out how the Index is obtained. But I still wasn't at the bull's eye. I had two questions: What is the exact wording of the five questions? What fraction of the replies tends to be neutral? The secretary told me, because my request involved proprietary information, I would be out of luck.

I wanted the exact wording of the five questions in order to find out how I would answer them. For instance, I haven't the faintest idea about business conditions six months from now. I also wanted to know the number of neutral replies because, if it is large, then the sample that matters may be much less than 3500, hence less reliable.

Even with 3500 responses, which is, statistically speaking, a good-size sample, there is a range of possible sampling error. "Sampling error" is the term statisticians use for the random variations you get when you use the responses from a random sample to estimate what you would find had you been able to survey the whole population. This error may easily be larger than one percent.

When the August index is reported as 94.5, it may be one percent larger or smaller; that is, anywhere from 94.5 + 0.945 (about 95.4) to 94.5 – 0.945 (about 93.6) Similarly, when the September index is 93.3, it could be anywhere between 92.4 and 94.2. This diagram shows the possible ranges:

The reported August Consumer Confidence Index is 94.5. That for Septenber is 93.5, but the error bars overlap, so there is a chance that consumer confidence went up, not down.

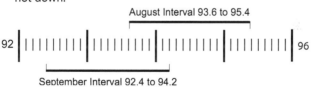

August Interval 93.6 to 95.4

September Interval 92.4 to 94.2

A glance comparing the August and September possibilities shows that, instead of the decline suggested by this particular sample, there might have been a rise in consumer confidence in the population as a whole from August to September; the index could have gone from 93.6 to 94.2. Maybe consumers were ready to spend, spend, spend.

The change in the index in one month, usually small, may be due completely to unavoidable errors in sampling. The Conference Board advises the financial world to consider the index only over a period of several months and only in conjunction with other information, but the temptation to react to the change in numbers, especially if their origins are mysterious, is hard to resist.

A NUMBER ABOUT THE FUTURE

While browsing through the handbook, I came upon a section on the Index of Leading Economic Indicators, a number that is supposed to foretell the behavior of the economy. I had wondered for a long time where this number, which is also released monthly, comes from.

I had no idea how I would devise a way to provide such an index. Maybe I could count the number of boxcars that pass by on the tracks about a mile from my home. They would tend to carry bulky items, which would go into finished products a few months later. Years ago economists did keep track of boxcar loadings, perhaps for the same reason.

As expected, the Conference Board has a much more sensible and complex method. I will describe their technique in detail. However, you may not want to know what it is for the same reason that you don't want to know what goes into a sausage.

First, several sources give the Board data in ten areas of the economy. From the Census Bureau they obtain Manufacturers' New Orders for Consumer Goods, Manufacturers' New Orders for Non-defense Capital Goods, and Building Permits for New Private Housing Units. From the Bureau of Labor, they get data on average weekly hours in manufacturing and weekly claims for unemployment insurance.

The Federal Reserve provides an estimate of the money supply and the difference between the interest rates on a 10-year Treasury bond and the overnight interbank borrowing rate. The National Association of Purchasing Management provides a number that describes the relative speed with which industries received deliveries from their suppliers. Standard and Poor's records the behavior of 500 selected common stocks, while the University of Michigan contributes an index of consumer expectations.

Most of these numbers are subject to the usual sampling errors. However, I doubt that the error in average weekly hours is large, since it is based on questionnaires sent to 300,000 firms and has a response rate, after two reminders, of 80 percent.

Next, the Conference Board measures the change during a month in each of the ten numbers. For a component that is just a percent, the change is simply the difference between the percents at the beginning and at the end of the month. For other components, the arithmetic is more involved in finding the percentage change in a month.

If the number at the beginning of the month is A and at the end is B, the change is B – A. No surprise there. One would expect the Board then to divide this by A to get the relative change during the month, but that is not what they do. Instead they divide B – A by the average of A and B, namely by (A + B)/2. One can think of this as the average reading during the whole month. For instance, if A is 6 and B is 8, then their average is 7, and the quotient, "the difference between 6 and 8, divided by the average of 6 and 8," becomes 2/7 or roughly 0.29, which is 29 percent.

At this point in the calculation there are ten percentages. One might expect the Board to average these ten numbers by adding them all up and dividing by ten. This amounts to giving all the numbers equal weights of one tenth, which is ten hundredths, or 0.10.

This is not what the Board does. Some of the categories tend to have wilder month-to-month fluctuations than others. To compensate for this, they weight each category, with the more wild components given smaller weights. These weights vary from 0.0125 to 0.3274 and are adjusted annually. For instance, if the increase in some category is 2 percent and the weight is 0.3274, the adjusted number is 0.6548.

The ten different weighted percents are recorded to two decimal places and then summed. That number is viewed as the percent change in the index in one month. Call it "s."

Now the calculation gets even more hairy. You can skip the details, but just note that a lot of computation is involved in finding the number that is supposed to measure the state of business six months in advance. If you remember your first-year high-school algebra, you can follow their reasoning. However, if your eyes glaze over when you see an equation with letters, just take a quick glance to get a feeling for how fancy the calculation is.

The Conference Board then computes the new index in terms of the preceding month's index and the percentage change. If the old index is A and the new one will be B, then they demand that the change, $B - A$, when divided by the average of A and $B,$ be $s/100$. (They must divide by 100 since s is expressed as a percent. Thus 50 percent becomes $1/2$.) In other words, they know A and s, and want to find B in this equation:

$$\frac{B - A}{(B + A)/2} = \frac{s}{100}$$

A little high school algebra solves that equation for B.

For instance, if the change in one month is a dramatic $s = 50$ percent, you replace s by 50, solve the resulting equation for B, and find that B is $5/3$ times A. That is about 167 percent of A, a 67 percent increase — not the 50 percent you start with.

Rather paradoxical. However, the Board probably prefers to compare the change to the whole month rather than to the beginning of the month, as I mentioned.

The resulting number, called the Index of Leading Economic Indicators, is one of the tools used to predict where the economy will be in a few months: At an expansion? At a recession? In between?

One trouble in developing and testing such tools is that there have not been many peaks and troughs, at least not enough on which to base a theory. Another is that each has its own dynamic and duration. Also, it's hard to tell if there is a recession. Sometimes a group of economists must meet to decide whether there is or had been a recession and to decide the dates of its start and end. Moreover, during an alleged recession some sectors of the economy may be expanding while others are shrinking. After all, an economy is a multi-dimensional object, far more complicated than the shapes of triangles discussed in Chapter 12. It would be surprising if its behavior could be recorded by a single number.

Those obstacles should be contrasted with the comparatively simple challenge a chemist faces when determining the boiling point of water at sea level. First, there is no doubt when it boils.

Second, every time it boils the thermometer will show the same number, 212 degrees Fahrenheit.

As the economist Philip Klein admits, because of the unique aspect of every business cycle, "... a thoroughly adequate theory applicable to all business cycles is unattainable. It follows that a totally reliable set of indicators is equally unattainable."

Moreover the economy keeps changing. As the handbook notes, "The U.S. economy is continually evolving, and is too complex to be completely summarized by just a few statistics."

No wonder that predictions of where the economy is going have a mixed record.

The first index of leading indicators appeared in the 1930s. Since then, in spite of much tinkering, economists have discovered that it has not become a reliable predictor of peaks and valleys of the economy. Looking back in 1970, F. E. Morris remarked that the indicator had predicted "nine out of the last five recessions." Ten years later B. Molefsky lamented, "That policy makers do not apparently rely on the leading indicators to any large extent says a great deal about their utility."

In 1998, F.X. Diebold and G.D. Rudebusch in their book, *Business Cycles,* could still report,

> *Our work casts doubt on the effectiveness of what was often called 'the government's primary forecasting tool' and leads one to question what, if anything, the leading index leads... Since we delivered our pessimistic assessment of the track record of the index, the United States government has gotten out of the business, having transferred the rights to the Conference Board in the mid 1990's.*

The fate of this index, revised and fine-tuned for over six decades, may send a message that transcends the confines of economics. It reminds us that there well may be a limit on our ability to peer into the future, a limit as real as a brick wall, fine-tune our arithmetic as we may. The best we may do is accept that there is such a limit and try, somehow, to find what it is.

HOW ABOUT THE CPI?

Perhaps we can do without the Consumer Confidence Index and the Index of Leading Economic Indicators, but we cannot dump the Consumer Price Index, affectionately known as the CPI, which is a measure of inflation. This came on the scene during WW I, when inflation was very high and wages, especially in shipbuilding, had to be determined. The CPI is used in calculating benefits in Social Security and other pensions, in setting income tax brackets, and in escalation clauses reflecting the cost of living. No wonder the Bureau of Labor Statistics was ordered to come up with a single number with which to measure the cost of living.

Imagine trying to find such a number. You would have to monitor the cost of various goods and services. Which ones? How much should each be weighed? If the price of a box of breakfast cereal varies from store to store, which store should you use? Which cereal? How would you deal with new technology, such as the digital camera? What if an invention is so innovative, like the microwave oven, that it does not displace earlier contrivances?

Moreover, each family has its own cost of living. If you don't fly, you're not affected by a rise in the price of airline tickets. If you own your home, you're not concerned with an increase in rents. On the other hand, the elderly are very much aware of the cost of medicine. As my brother Mel wonders, " If there's no inflation, how can all the prices be going up so fast?"

It is no wonder that the CPI is a source of controversy. Every so often there's a news item, such as one headlined, "Index Overstates Inflation Rate." It begins,

> *A congressional commission reports that the governmental measure of inflation for the cost of living is overstated by 1 percent a year, enough to cost the United States Treasury billions of dollars a year in extra payments to Social Security and other benefit programs.*

Let's look at the numbers closely. Say that the Bureau of Labor Statistics asserts that the inflation rate is 2 percent, while the commission says it is 1 percent. That sounds like a wide discrepancy; one estimate is twice the other.

But watch how the 2 percent is calculated. It is the change in the index over a year, from 100 to 102, say. The commission says it should go to only 101 instead. The argument is not over one number being twice another, but over the difference between two numbers that are quite close to each other, 101 and 102.

It looks like someone is making a mountain out of a molehill. There may not even be a molehill if more than a 1 percent error in the sample may swallow the entire dispute. After all, two economists, using the same procedures for calculating the CPI, can easily arrive at numbers differing by more than 1 percent.

In spite of all these caveats, the nation needs a single number to be called "the cost of living." It is essential for maintaining domestic tranquility that most of us view it as meaningful and objective. When it makes its monthly appearance it should be treated with respect, just as a shaman's rain dance should be treated with respect by his tribe. For this reason it is important that we not worry about how it is calculated. All that matters is that we honor the CPI, which is far more crucial in the conduct of our lives than the circumference of the earth or the distance to the moon. Try to forget you ever read this chapter.

14   A Scale for Uncertainty

Two in the bush; Kick or run; Life is a lottery;
Gambles everywhere.

For four chapters I have posted warnings about the *abuse* of numbers. As someone whose career has been spent with them I am happy now to describe a case for the *use* of numbers. I'm not the first person to realize that numbers could help us make decisions. As we will see, workers in meteorology, the Central Intelligence Agency, and banking have already urged that numbers be introduced into predictions, a key part of decisions. For isn't any decision a statement about the future, either immediate or remote?

TWO IN THE BUSH?

When we choose between two goals we compare not only their values but also the likelihood that we will reach those goals. The same is true when we contemplate possible losses.

The saying, "A bird in the hand is worth two in the bush," illustrates this type of choice. But this advice to a hungry hunter is not as simple as it sounds. It depends on how accurate you are with a shotgun. If you are a sharpshooter, sure you would get both birds in the bush, then two in the bush are worth much more than a bird in the hand. If, on the other hand, you are likely to miss because of the excitement, then a bird in the hand is indeed worth more than two in the bush.

KICK OR RUN?

The same type of choice occurs in real life, even in sports. For instance, a football coach faces a similar problem after his team has scored a touchdown. His team can then score two points by either running or passing the ball into the end zone, starting at the two-yard line; or it can aim for just one point by kicking the ball through the goalposts.

In contrast to the case of the birds, neither choice is a sure thing. However, the coach knows how successful teams have been with each option. In the National Football League the one-point attempt has been a near certainty, scoring 94 percent of the time. The two-point strategy was much less successful, succeeding only 37 percent of the time.

To compare the two approaches, the coach could imagine using each one, say, one hundred times. The one-point choice would succeed about 94 of those times. On average, then, it produces .94 points per attempt. The two-point attempt would work only 37 times, for a total score of 74 points. On average, that is .74 points for each try. Early in the game it is wiser to take the more conservative route, even though it means earning only one point.

(Near the end of the game the choice becomes more complicated. Then the decision is influenced by the difference in the teams' scores and by the time left in the game. Statisticians have prepared cards for the coaches that suggest the better strategy in terms of time and scores.)

The coach could make the calculation more directly. He can just multiply .94 times 1 and .37 times 2, getting .94 and .74 right off the bat, without imagining the hundred trials. He can think of .94 as "the average number of points per kick" and .74 as "the average number of points per running or passing."

In short, *the coach can simply multiply two numbers.* One of the numbers describes the size of the possible gain. The other records the likelihood of success. Statisticians call this likelihood the "probability" of success, a number anywhere from 0 to 1. If one is absolutely sure of succeeding, the probability is 1, or one hundred percent. If there is no chance, the probability is 0.

LIFE IS A LOTTERY

The number you get when you multiply the possible gain by its probability is called your "expectation." The same notion applies to possible losses as well: you multiply the possible loss by the probability that it may occur.

Imagine playing a lottery whose prize is a million dollars and ten million tickets are sold. You buy one ticket, forking over one dollar. Your expectation is $1/10,000,000$ times $1,000,000 = 1/10$. (one ten-millionth of a million is a tenth.) That is one tenth of a dollar, or a mere dime. In this case, since your expectation is less than your cost, from a financial point of view the bet is unwise. However, as an entertainment it may justify itself by providing visions of instant wealth. If you made the same wager week after week, you would lose, on average, ninety cents per week. In ten million tries you would probably hit the jackpot once.

If, instead, only a million tickets are sold, your expectation would be larger, namely $1/1,000,000$ times $1,000,000$, which is 1, since all the zeros cancel out.

Your expectation is now one dollar, exactly what the bet costs. Now the wager is a fair bet. This means that in the long run you would tend to just about break even. In a million runs of the lottery you would expect to win once, collecting a million dollars. Alas, during that time you would also have spent a million dollars for the tickets.

Going back to the birds, let us compute some expectations. Say that you will bag the two birds in the bush 60 percent of the time. Your expectation for this choice is then $.60 \times 2 = 1.2$ birds. The expectation for the case of choosing the bird in the hand, since the probability is 1, is simply

$1 \times 1 = 1$ bird.

So trying to get the birds in the bush is the better choice over the long run. However, if you are facing starvation and one bird is all you need to save your life, then it is better to choose the bird in the hand.

The key to calculating an expectation is the number that records the probability. There are two ways to estimate this number in some cases.

If the situation you face resembles situations that you or others have dealt with before, then you can use the accumulated information to estimate the probability. The football coach can do this. So can meteorologists, who can look back at similar weather conditions to make their predictions. Studies of the performance of experienced meteorologists show that when they make a prediction such as, "There is a forty percent chance of rain tomorrow," it rains in about forty percent of the cases. Expert bridge players also can estimate quite well the probabilities that various cards will appear.

Another way to estimate a probability is theoretical. For instance, the probability that a penny turns up heads when tossed is one half, since heads and tails are equally likely. You can calculate the odds in games of chance, such as roulette, similarly.

GAMBLES EVERYWHERE

But in many decisions, either personal or public, neither method is available. For instance, the CIA in 1970, when planning to block Allende from being elected the head of Chile, estimated that "Viaux did not have more than one chance in twenty — perhaps less — to launch a successful coup."

Paul Volcker, former chairman of the Federal Reserve, said in 2004 that there is a 75% chance of a financial crisis by the year 2009. He wouldn't have been surprised by the mortgage and gasoline crisis of 2008.

Steven Chu, a Nobel laureate, believes that by the year 2100 global warming will shrink the Sierra Nevada snow pack, a major source of fresh water: "There's a two-thirds chance there will be a disaster and that's in the best scenario."

John Kennedy, looking back on the Cuban Missile Crisis, estimated that the odds that the Soviets would go to war seemed "somewhere between one out of three and even." But what does a phrase such as "one out of three" mean?

Perhaps, it means that if on three separate occasions we meet the very same conditions as Kennedy did in Cuba, one of them would trigger a war. Of course, since situations like that missile crisis are never repeated identically, this definition is impractical.

Maybe "one out of three" just describes the degree of Kennedy's confidence in his belief that there would be a war. These two interpretations may be saying the same thing.

There is a third possible meaning, one which has the advantage that it can be verified scientifically. A prediction of "one in three" could be short for "if you check all my predictions in which I say 'one in three,' you will find that about a third come true." That is how we check the skill of a seasoned meteorologist.

No one can be certain how the future will unfold. Decisions and plans involve gambles. That means that probabilities are lurking in the background, even though we may not want to draw attention to them. We don't like to think like insurance companies, who deal with risk and odds head-on. Nor do we want to picture ourselves as living in a big casino with roulette wheels spinning and dice tumbling across a table.

Sherman Kent, a legendary CIA analyst, who retired in 1967, believed that the numerical odds should accompany intelligence estimates offered to policy clients. In *Sherman Kent and the Profession of Intelligence Analysis*, Jack Davis wrote:

> *He thought that American policy officials all understood the meaning of frequently cited odds favoring one or another sports team and that substantive uncertainty could effectively be expressed with similar expressions. He had the following argument with one of his chief deputies, who preferred verbal estimation depictions (good chance, real possibility, strong likelihood) that Kent deplored as more colorful than meaningful.*

> Said R. Jack Smith: *Sherm, I don't like what I see in our recent papers. A 2-to-1 chance of this; 50-50 odds on that. You are turning us into the biggest bookie shop in town.*

Replied Kent: *R. J., I'd rather be a bookie than a [blank-blank] poet.*

The CIA did not adopt Kent's suggestion. Instead, it uses phrases such as "we judge with high confidence," "we assess with low confidence," and "we judge with moderate confidence," even in framing a national intelligence estimate for the President. There must be enough such assessments for some historically minded scholar to read them all, and figure out the accuracy rate of each of the three types. Without such a study, who could possibly know what the words "high," "low," and, "moderate" mean?

Robert Rubin, Secretary of the Treasury under President Clinton, learned early to think of the future in terms of the odds.

At Harvard and at Yale Law School, I learned to think about uncertainties and the ambiguities of life intellectually. When I got to Goldman Sachs, I learned it was a matter of financial life and death to learn to be probabilistic. If you thought in absolutes of black-and-whites, sooner or later you got wiped out. The odds would catch up with you.

Imagine that a deal has an eighty percent chance of going through and making a profit of three dollars per share. The "upside potential" is then

.80 x 3 = $2.40.

But the deal has a twenty percent risk of collapsing, in which case it will lose eight dollars a share. The "downside risk" is then

.20 x 8 = $1.60.

The total expectation per share is then upside potential minus the downside risk = $2.40 – $1.60 = 80 cents. Since the expectation is positive, the deal may be tempting.

There is a catch in the calculation. The trouble lies in the probabilities. Where do they come from? Not from theory. Not from comparison with many similar cases, since each deal is a fresh gamble.

Rubin estimated these likelihoods based on his best judgment, sharpened over the years. This kind of probability is called "subjective probability." The psychologists Amos Tversky and Daniel Kahneman, who spent decades studying subjective estimates of odds, concluded that they are not reliable. Even so, they are worth making.

For instance, Rubin, by calling attention to the uncertainty, raised it to a topic to be considered and debated. Introducing numbers at least may subdue excessive optimism and call attention to the grey area between black and white. A treasury aide recalled, "He asked me if a bill would make it through Congress and I said 'absolutely.' He didn't like that one bit. Now I say the probability is 60 percent — and we argue about whether it's 59 or 60."

That is quite a contrast with the way we usually think and talk. When we are pushing a project we imply that it will surely unfold as planned. We treat it as though the probability of success is 100 percent.

Of course there are words that describe, however vaguely, the various levels of likelihood, such as "certain," "almost certain," "very likely," "probable," "even-steven," "unlikely," "improbable," and "impossible." Since in a heated debate one should sound certain, not wishy-washy, one avoids these subtler distinctions. Using numbers instead of words to describe the degree of certainty may help change the tone of a discussion. We may ask a very confident participant, "What would you say are the odds that your scheme will work, and how did you decide on those odds?"

That does more than help clarify the deliberations and cool overheated confidence. With the vast memory now available in modern computers, we could keep a better record of the accuracy of our leaders' predictions. That would provide some measure of their grasp on reality. Doing this, however, would mean that we take life as seriously as we do sports. When you browse through the sports pages you enter a jungle of numbers. During the baseball season, you can check players' batting averages to three decimal places. In the football season, you can find for each quarterback the percent of passes completed. For basketball, there is the fraction of attempts that go through the hoop.

It is odd that we monitor our sports heroes much more closely than we do our leaders, even our president. That is consistent with our supplying umpires at a game, but leaving the contest between nations an unregulated madhouse.

There are bloggers who keep tabs on a few pundits. As a result, we have a new unit of time, a "Friedman unit," which stands for "the next six months." It honors the pundit, Thomas Friedman, whose comments on the Iraq occupation for years promised that within the next six months we will know such and such, which is a safe way to appear wise. Once a pundit, forever a pundit.

We could develop a data bank at least for the few hundred individuals at the top of our government, though it would not be as easy as following the performance of a pitcher or quarterback. But I am sure we will not try. It isn't just because our leaders' statements are much harder to check. There is a much deeper reason, but that is a matter we will take up later, when I explore the complex relation between us outsiders and those we call "experts."

15 It Will Definitely Happen, Perhaps

Many investigations; Don't turn prophecy into a science.

We have managed to turn alchemy into chemistry and astrology into astronomy, but the field of prophecy remains as primitive as it was in ancient Egypt. In the big decisions the predictions usually are "it will happen" or "it won't happen." There are no gradations between those extremes, especially in the heat of debate.

We claim with as much confidence as we can project either an event will certainly occur or it certainly will not. The grey zone between those extremes disappears. It's as if we are using a thermometer with only two number, 212 for boiling and 32 for freezing. Meteorologists, chemists, or chefs working with the aid of such a limited scale would hardly be able to practice their professions. Yet that is what we do when we make our predictions. We are remarkably casual about the art of forecasting.

As mentioned in the last chapter, Rubin urged decision makers to attach a number to a prediction to indicate the likelihood that the prediction will be fulfilled. He wanted them to keep in mind the uncertainty of the future. Kent, on the other hand, wanted analysts to couch their predictions numerically in order to communicate more accurately with the officials who depend on the CIA's intelligence estimates. I wrote to the CIA, asking if it implemented Kent's suggestion, made over forty years ago.There was no reply.

The National Weather Service does use numbers in describing the probability of precipitation, PoP. Their code: "slight chance or widely scattered" is 20 percent; "chance or scattered" is 30, 40, or 50 percent; "likely or numerous" is 60 or 70 percent; and "occasional or periods" is 80, 90, or 100 percent.

MANY INVESTIGATIONS

Though numbers generally don't accompany predictions, there has been a great deal of study of the contrast of verbal and numerical estimates of likelihood. The research, which spans half a century, appears in a wide variety of journals, such as *Organizational Behavior and Human Decision Processes, Business Forecasting. Risk and Uncertainty, Medical Decision Making, Management Science, Risk Analysis,* and *International Journal of Approximate Reasoning.* There are also countless books with similar titles. Among the many researchers are R. Beyth-Marom, D.V.Budescu, B. Fischhoff, D.Kahneman, S. Lichtentstein, P.Tversky, and T.S. Wallstein.

Ray Simpson published the first study, in 1944. While working on the paper, he talked with an eye specialist, who complained that a book on diseases of the eye used "words of too great elasticity in meaning," such as "frequently," "may occur," "usually," and "rare." Simpson discovered that the term, "rather often," "to some individuals means less than 40 percent of the time, while to others it is likely to mean over 80 percent." He asked 335 high school, college, and graduate students to tell what percents they would attach to various words in a long list. For example, he found that there was general agreement on the meaning of "almost never" but not on the meaning of "frequently."

In an investigation in 1967 called *Empirical Scaling of Common Verbal Phrases Associated with Numerical Probabilities,* Lichtenstein and Newman asked people to translate the words "probable" and "seldom" into numbers. The range of responses to "probable" extended from 1 percent to 99 percent, an amazing spread, while those to "seldom" went from 1 percent to 47 percent. At least "seldom" did tend to be seen as less likely than "probable." The wide range in both cases shows how vague are the words we use when we make plans.

In the first volume of the *Journal of Forecasting*, which appeared in 1982, Beyth-Marom reported the results of a similar study in *How Probable is Probable? A Numerical Translation of Verbal Probability Expressions.* This research was conducted not among amateurs but in a professional forecasting organization accustomed to using words to describe probabilities. Even so, the range of responses to the verbal descriptions of likelihood was alarmingly wide. After tossing out the lowest ten percent and the highest ten percent as being atypical, she found that the range remained large. These are the results for a few of the expressions, with extreme responses removed.

"Not likely" drew responses from 2 percent to 18 percent. "Chances are not great" elicited higher odds, anywhere from 22 percent to 52 percent. "It seems to me" produced estimates from 50 percent to 73 percent.

The numerical interpretations of the thirty expressions used in the experiment were divided into seven levels, with "not likely" being level 1 and "certain" being level 7.

Here are the seven categories. In each category I include a number in parentheses that suggests the corresponding probability.

1. Not likely, very low chance, poor chance (10% chance)

2. Doubtful, low chance, small chance (20% chance)

3. Can't rule out entirely, chances are not great, perhaps (40% chance)

4. Not inevitable, one must consider, may, possible (50% chance)

5. It could be, likely, it seems, non-negligible chance, one can expect, reasonable to assume, it seems to me, one could assume, reasonable chance, meaningful chance (60% chance)

6. High chance, most likely, close to certain (80% chance)

7. Nearly certain, very high chance, certain (90% chance).

That is the result of presenting the phrases in isolation, not as part of specific predictions. The experiment continued by presenting the expressions as they appeared in predictions made by the organization. The results were similar, with broad numerical translations for the phrases as wide as when they were offered without a context.

DON'T TURN PROPHECY INTO A SCIENCE

As long as the words we use in dealing with the future are so vague, there is little chance of evaluating forecasters. That may be why forecasters are loath to shift from words to numbers. As long as we are content to use words to describe probabilities we will make slow progress, if any, in turning forecasting into a science. Perhaps, subconsciously, we laypersons already believe that there can be no progress: the future is such a tangled web of interacting choices, passions, and inventions that there is no hope in figuring out what is yet to unfold.

There may be still another reason. A leader can now say, for instance, "We will invade and the war will be short." That has a strong emotional pull, redolent of bugles and drums. It is a call to arms with the built-in certainty of a promise. But translate it first to, "We will invade, and I think the war will be short." Already a bit of its charm fades. Then go to, "We will invade and I think there is a high chance that the war will be short," and finally to, "We will invade and I think there is an 80 percent chance that the war will be short." By the time the prediction reaches this state, it hardly serves as a rousing call to arms. The appeal has moved step by step from the emotional to the analytic, from the reptilian brain to the cortex. Someone hearing it will start to worry about the 20 percent chance of a long war and ask what the phrases "short war" and "long war" mean. By that stage the leader's enthusiasm would lose its punch, the invasion is cancelled, and we all return to our peacetime pursuits.

It makes practical sense to introduce numbers, if only to emphasize the uncertainty implicit in our actions that must play out in a world that exists only in our imagination. If a reporter at a press conference would ask the big shot behind the podium to put the predictions in numbers, doing so could become a custom. At first the exchange between big shot and reporter may run like this:

Big Shot: *It will happen.*

Reporter: *Are you absolutely sure?*

Big Shot: *A slip between the cup and the lip is always possible.*

Reporter: *Then you're not absolutely sure.*

Big Shot: *I'm as certain as a mere mortal can be.*

Reporter: *How uncertain are you?*

Big Shot: *You're heckling me. There is scarcely any chance of failure.*

Reporter: *Would you say you are about 80 percent sure?*

Big Shot: *That's about right.*

Reporter: *We'll put that in our computer along with all your other predictions, and check up on it later.*

Big Shot: *No one's perfect.*

With experience, this conversation would be replaced with the brief statement by the Big Shot, "There is an 80 percent chance it will happen." And we will absorb it the way we hear that there is a 40 percent chance of rain tomorrow. In that case, we will be joining Robert Rubin, John Kennedy, and Sherman Kent. If the custom deprives the insider of charisma, that's all to the good.

If we don't make this shift as a tribe, then at least we could do so on our own, just to get the feel of it. This shift will ensure that we take every pronouncement with a grain of salt and that we adjust the size of the grain to the record of the pundit making it. This practice would help close the gap between us outsiders and the insiders.

16 Just Try to Measure It

Whatever, put a number to it; Numbers in Government; Playing with the interest rate.

As I mentioned earlier, a choice would be simple if we could reduce it to deciding which of several numbers is the largest. Then we could avoid the choice between incomparables. However, as I warned in several chapters, there are obstacles that prevent numbers from extricating us from that dilemma. We are usually left to make a choice on the basis of what we call "wisdom," "judgment," or "experience."

Even so, circumstance may compel us to quantify the seemingly unquantifiable.

WHATEVER, PUT A NUMBER ON IT

How much is wilderness worth? That question pops up when the government decides whether to allow mining, lumbering, or drilling in an area designated a wilderness. Some would say the price is infinite, others that it cannot be assigned a monetary value. Yet others would say that, since it supports an industry selling $18 billion a year of tents, camping equipment, food, clothing, climbing gear, fishing tackle, and so on, that wilderness can be assigned a price.

In making a complex decision by the cost-benefit method, great care is taken to quantify each cost and benefit, even though some values will successfully resist the charm of numbers. I will describe two major efforts.

The British government in 1968 appointed a commission to recommend a site for a third London airport, which, as it turns out, has yet to be built. Three years later, the commission published its recommendation in a report that showed how it used cost-benefit accounting.

It considered such incomparables as the cost of construction, travel time from the airport to London, noise pollution, jobs created or lost, houses destroyed, communities disrupted, open space, and historical buildings. In order to compare the costs and benefits of the various options, they quantified as much as they could. The cost of construction was the easiest. Others required a mix of assumptions.

This is how they estimated the cost of travel to London. The calculation required several steps. First, they estimated the number of business travelers who would use the airport. Then they estimated their annual incomes, translated to so much money per hour. Finally, they conjectured how long it would take to get from the airport to London. Putting these all together, they calculated the income lost in transit, which became part of the cost.

But they were never able to put a cost figure on the "churches that have survived centuries of civil war, vandalism, religious reformers, restorers, foreign foes, to be laid waste in the desire for swift travel by air."

As anticipated, the recommendation was controversial. A member of the commission, Colin Buchanan, wrote a twelve-page dissent at the end of the report. His main criticism was of the cost-benefit approach itself:

"I do not quarrel with the principle of costing separate items in order to compare the sites in respect to those items. Thus, given a consistent basis for the valuation of *business time*, then the figures give a comparison between the sites for business time costs.

"Again, accepting the figures for costing *noise nuisance*, then those figures give a comparison between the sites for noise.

"I get into difficulties over the aggregation of the costs to produce a 'batting order.' The whole cost-benefit approach has been pushed too far beyond the easily quantified problems that are its usual domain."

Once again, the problem of reconciling several incomparables, even if each one could be measured, made its inevitable unwelcome appearance, The value of a potential airport site could not be told by a single number.

If we mix flour, eggs, sugar, butter, milk, and chocolate, we end up with a cake. But if we mix incomparables, we end up with a concoction beyond the edge of reason. And we do it all the time.

NUMBERS IN GOVERNMENT

When he arrived from the Ford Motor Company to become Secretary of Defense in 1961, Robert McNamara introduced a refined version of cost-benefit accounting to the Department. Its acronym PPBS stood for *Planning, Programming, Budgeting System.* President Johnson in 1965 ordered it to be used in all executive departments.

Some nine hundred economists, mathematicians, and statisticians were hired to implement the method. Given a goal described by a policy maker, these masters of numbers would think of various programs that might achieve that goal and then calculate the benefit and cost for each one. They tried to bring as much of the program as they could within the grasp of numbers, just as that British commission did, leaving subjective values to the policy makers. This approach was to replace the conventional method, which just listed cost as a line item in a budget, not showing the relation between expenditure and purpose.

This arrangement led to a battle over turf, with the politicians afraid that the number crunchers were making policy decisions. Consequently, the Subcommittee on National Security and International Relations of the United States Senate held hearings on PPBS in 1968. The testimony was published in a 687-page book, which revealed the fears about the method.

Klaus Knorr, a professor of international relations, observed that there is a limit to what might be called an orderly approach: "To the extent that costs and benefits cannot be measured accurately, and to the extent that the problem is one of deciding, in an inherently subjective manner, problems of choice are unsusceptible to rigorous economic analysis."

Arthur Ross, Commissioner of Labor Statistics, reminded the committee of the role of intuition: "Specious quantification of the unquantifiable can be as mischievous as ignoring it. The peculiar genius of the human brain is that it can deal with qualitative issues. There is no substitute for the intuitive feel of a problem resulting from first-hand exposure to it."

These comments echo one of our recurrent themes, that there are limits on how wise we can be in planning the future and how deeply we can probe our own thought processes. That is what terms such as "inherently subjective," "peculiar genius," and "intuitive feel" suggest. The decision of the policy maker may depend on ideology, on personal loyalty, or on how long to the next election. It is not determined simply by facts and numbers considered in isolation.

James Schlesinger, a consultant on national security, commented that,

> The more political a study, the less likely is it to be pure. The process can be (and has been) far more corrupted, when phony numbers are introduced.
>
> For such goals as deterrence, controlled nuclear warfare, or welfare benefits, we fall back, not on a firm technical base, but on what may be scientific mush. The difficulty is sometimes dealt with by referring euphemistically to "the model problem."

Once again we are reminded of the modeling described in Chapter 1, with its diagram of the thirty lines. The mushiness of the model provides a fertile environment for mushy thought.

But the record of the hearings also includes criticism of PPBS on a more technical level, as I illustrate by the treatment of the interest rate.

PLAYING WITH THE INTEREST RATE

One element in a typical calculation is the future interest rate, which is used to estimate the value today of a promise of a certain number of dollars, say, ten years in the future. That number is the key to calculating the value today of future income from a project. A dollar ten years from now is worth less than a dollar today. Economists call its value today its "present value."

To see how this number is calculated, imagine that you open a bank account that pays interest each year, which is added to your account. Gradually the account grows. Assume that you want there to be $1000 in it in ten years.

If the bank were stingy and paid no interest, you would have to deposit $1000 now. On the other hand, if the bank were very generous, you would have to deposit much less than $1000. The amount you would deposit depends on the interest rate. The lower the interest rate, the more you would be obliged to deposit; the higher, the less you would have to. Whatever you must deposit would be called "the present value of $1000 delivered ten years from now."

Before the era of computers, there were printed tables displaying present values for a variety of interest rates. Now software or even a handheld calculator provides the information.

Alas, the interest rate fluctuates and no one knows what it will be ten years or even a year from now.

By *assuming* a low rate of interest, a planner magnifies the present value of a future income, such as that from electricity generated at a dam. Aaron Wildavsky, a professor of political science, illustrated how sensitive that estimate is to the assumed interest rate:

> *If the Corps of Engineers raised their [assumed] inter-*
> *est rate from 2 5/8 to 4, 6, or 8 percent, then 9, 64,*
> *and 80 percent of their projects, respectively, would*
> *have had a benefit-cost ratio of less than unity.*

The ratio being "less than unity" means that the benefit would be less than the cost, and the project would probably not have been undertaken. Someone opposed to the project would use a higher interest rate, to shrink the benefit.

Here is a concrete case: consider the effect of the assumed future interest rate on the health of U. S. Airways' pension plan. The government, using an interest rate standard for insurance companies, chose 5.1 percent. The company wanted to use a figure closer to 12 percent, based on returns during the previous seventeen years, a period of an expansive bull market. According to the government, the pension fund should have $3.4 billion on hand now in order to meet future obligations. By the airline calculations, using the higher interest rate, the present value of its obligation would be only $2.1 billion.

The retirement fund must fund retirements that will begin decades into the future, and no one can be sure how the interest rate will vary. But the regulators and company officials do not have the luxury of waiting years to learn its behavior. They must decide now whether the funds on hand are adequate.

The federal government abandoned PPBS in 1971, and "PPBS" has become a pejorative term. However, some of its methods survive at various levels of government.

In Executive Order 12866, published in the Federal Register in 1993, we come upon this advice in the spirit of PBBS:

> *Agencies should assess all costs and benefits of regulatory alternatives... Costs and benefits shall ...include both quantifiable measures (to the fullest extent that these can be usefully estimated) and qualitative measures of costs and benefits that are difficult to quantify, but nevertheless essential to consider. Further, in choosing among alternative ... approaches, agencies should select those that maximize net benefits (including potential economic, environmental, public health and safety, and other advantages.)*

At first glance, these recommendations seem to tie an agency's hands. However, when we think of the dramatic shifts in regulations when the administration in Washington changes, we see that the Executive Order leaves open a wide range of options.

These two examples —the airport commission and PPBS — show that when decision makers try to arrive at a choice methodically, making an effort to reduce all concerns to numbers, even central issues will elude their grasp.

We can expect that any choice of sufficient complexity, whether made by an individual or by a group, will have its subjective element, which escapes quantification, and invites controversy. The decision will be unpredictable, dependent upon the particular circumstance of the moment and on whoever happens to be in a position to decide.

17   The GRIMP

Some simple arithmetic; The saga of a GRIMP;
The biggest GRIMP.

About twenty miles west of me in the Coast Range stands the Berryessa Dam, which holds back a lake over ten miles long. If a major earthquake demolished it, the escaping water could reach my town. Even so, I haven't bought a boat. If the little town of Winters, which is much closer to the dam, is busily adding new houses, why should I worry? I go about my daily affairs paying no attention to the hypothetical disaster. Nor have I bought earthquake insurance though ominous letters advise me that I am gambling with fate.

My situation is different from that of the inhabitants of New Orleans before Katrina struck. They had been told that it was just a matter of time before one of the many hurricanes would come near enough to overwhelm their levees and flood the city. They were aware the worst-case scenario would come to pass some day, and managed to live with this knowledge.

We all get from one day to the next in spite of the fear that something very big can go dreadfully wrong. An unfortunate bit of arithmetic shows why we have no other recourse once the die is cast.

SOME SIMPLE ARITHMETIC

Imagine yourself trying to estimate the "downside risk" of a gigantic enterprise that has a negligible chance of failure, although such a failure would involve a huge loss of life or property. It could be a dam, a chemical plant, or even thousands of nuclear-tipped missiles.

Using the statisticians' technique of calculating expectation, as practiced by Robert Rubin or the football coach, you multiply two numbers: the probability that the feared disaster might occur, and the size of the disaster, measured in lives lost or the dollar cost. The probability of its happening is a small number, near 0, while the possible loss is represented by a large number. We use our "best judgment" to estimate those two numbers.

But we also face a question about elementary arithmetic. What happens when you multiply a small number by a large number? The answer is "just about anything" as a few examples will show.

Recall that a billion is a thousand millions and that a million is a thousand thousands.

Now, one-billionth times one million is 1/1000, since a billion is a thousand times as large as a million. So, in this case, a small number times a large one is small.

But one millionth times one billion is 1000, which we may think of as large. Finally, one millionth times one million is 1, a middling sort of number.

With the aid of trillions and trillionths we could make the product of a small number and a large number much larger or smaller. In any case, the examples show why the product of a small number and a big one can be whatever we would like it to be.

We may have some idea of the size of the loss in a worst possible scenario, but what about estimating the probability that that loss will ever occur? There lies the heart of the problem. Now that our enterprises have grown so large and complex, we often encounter this conundrum. Like some problems in mathematics, it seems to be unsolvable. The very novelty of our creations deprives us of a way to estimate the likelihood that they will fail. This is the case with the "perfect storm" of new financial instruments combined with skullduggery that brought the recession that began in 2008.

But events in the natural world, even if they have hundreds of precedents, can elude our analysis. After a multi-page analysis, geologists in 1999 announced that there was a 70% chance of an earthquake of magnitude at least 6.7 in the San Francisco Bay Area by 2030. But two statisticians, D.A. Freeman and P.B. Stark, examined the reasoning and concluded:

> *Many steps involve models that are largely untestable; modeling choices often seem arbitrary. Another large earthquake in the Bay Area is inevitable, and imminent in geologic time. Probabilities are a distraction. Instead of making forecasts, the USGS could help improve building codes and plan the government's response to the next large earthquake. People should secure water heaters and bookcases and ignore the forecast.*

Good advice for preparing for any grand disaster, which has little chance of taking place today or tomorrow.

Our world must nevertheless deal with the "GRIMP," which stands for the "Gigantic Risk with Incredibly Minute Probability."

THE SAGA OF A GRIMP

The plot of the GRIMP has a form as well defined as a western movie or a murder mystery. For example, an earthen dam is built in spite of the protests of those who warn it is unsafe. Its advocates are typically full-time professionals. Its critics are mostly laypersons protesting in their spare time, perhaps with the aid of a few whistleblowers formerly employed by the dam builders. These protesters are usually dubbed "Luddites" or "activists" by the advocates.

The first epithet, which puts the opponents on the defensive, suggests that they are against progress. The second implies that their private lives are so dull that they get involved in public affairs in order to add a little excitement. Indeed, "activist" verges on "hyperactive," a disturbance treated by psychotropic pills. It implies that the main goal of the opponents is to be busy. If they didn't oppose the dam, they would oppose a dump, a prison, or a foster care home, whatever. They wouldn't be *for* anything.

The advocates, on the other hand, appear objective, with their insights based on unbiased studies. However, their livelihood and career depend on pushing the project through. Usually they dress better than the critics, most likely wearing a tie, which enhances their credibility. The critics, though they have no hidden axe to grind, no conflict of interest, no financial investment at risk, appear subjective, emotional, fearful Chicken Littles.

Years pass, and the dam holds firm. With each additional year the dam stands, with each downpour it survives, its critics look more foolish and its advocates more astute. Then, undermined by seepage, the dam collapses, inflicting great damage and loss of life in the valley below.

An official panel is appointed to find out how the disaster came to pass. Its final report, which comes out a year later, confirms the warnings of the critics, some of whom, ironically, may have drowned when the dam collapsed. Investigative reporters reveal that some employees of the company that built the dam had from the beginning expressed the same fears as the activists. The only comfort of the surviving activists is being able to say, "I told you so."

That is the tale of the Teton Dam in southeastern Idaho, which collapsed on June 5, 1976. It is the typical scenario of the GRIMP that ends in disaster.

An accident less severe than the ultimate catastrophe complicates the plot. The proponents can point out that their project survived, just as they had predicted. The larger this accident, the closer it came to the ultimate, the more it challenged the system, the more secure the enterprise must be.

The opponents argue that the accident shows that the odds that the ultimate catastrophe will some day occur are larger than anyone had earlier thought: Therefore, we should shut the project down while we are still ahead. The two sides illustrate clearly the principle of the perceptual option and the key role of the model.

After the Three Mile Island nuclear reactor meltdown, a proponent wrote, "The accident supports the view that nuclear reactors are safe, since it represents the loss of coolant situation that nuclear critics fear. The reactor did not melt down."

The critics saw the partial meltdown, which designers of the reactor had described as extremely unlikely, as evidence that a total meltdown is not as remote a possibility as had been described.

After an accident at a GRIMP some modification is made. The scenario starts to unroll again from scratch, but at a higher level of confidence on one side and of trepidation on the other. This diagram, which shows the sense of safety as a function of time, describes the evolution of a GRIMP that ends in disaster.

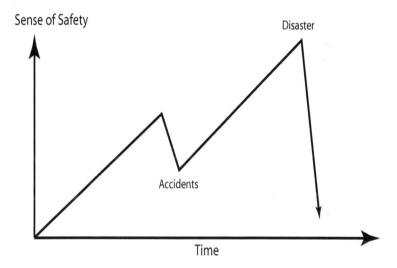

Of course, the project may never fail, but there is no way of knowing that. To find out, we build it and wait and watch to see what will happen.

The nuclear reactors in France, which produce most of its electricity, have had no major problems. Perhaps this is a GRIMP that will not end in disaster. In this case the graph of the "sense of safety" will rise forever, as shown here.

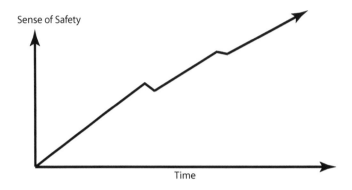

The buildup of carbon dioxide in the atmosphere and possible global warming is another GRIMP. If it occurs, oceans may inundate coastal cities, deserts consume fertile land, and parched forests turn to kindling.

The GRIMP is a special case of what planners call "the known unknown," in contrast to "the unknown unknown," which is totally unanticipated. Nassim Taleb, in *The Black Swan,* confronted that threat to our best-laid plans. But for me, the GRIMP provides worry enough.

The biggest GRIMP of all is hardly ever mentioned. Though it is worldwide it is invisible. It needs no lobbyists, and activists have a hard time spreading their message of alarm. It is the thousands of nuclear bombs, both atomic and thermonuclear, resting on missiles or stored. I worried about those bombs at the height of the Cold War. And I worry about them now in a changed world.

THE BIGGEST GRIMP

To give some sense of these bombs, consider that the radius of destruction of a hand grenade is five feet, that of the Oklahoma City bomb is 330 feet, of a 15000-pound "iron" or "gravity" bomb, 2000 feet, but of a 10 megaton H-bomb, 15 miles. A single atom bomb can destroy a medium-size city, while an H-bomb can obliterate the largest metropolitan area. The radioactive plume from such bombs spreads death to unpredictable distances. The fallout from what is called a "nuclear exchange" (for "war" would be a euphemism) could precipitate a planetary disaster unequaled except perhaps by the one that ended the reign of the dinosaurs. I try to imagine it by visualizing a million collapsing World Trade Centers against a background of leveled Hiroshima and flooded New Orleans backlit by endless forest fires. Even throwing in all the earthquakes that have ever occurred, I'm sure that image is still inadequate.

This GRIMP has haunted us ever since the bombs of August, 1945. Within three months the naval historian Bernard Brodie argued in a 28-page memorandum that the only reasonable use of the atomic bomb is as a deterrent, to prevent its use by anyone else:

> It may prove in the net a powerful inhibition to aggression. It would make little difference if one power had more bombs and were better prepared to resist them than the opponent. It would in any case undergo tremendous destruction of life and property.

Over the years geopoliticians and armchair warriors have tried to wiggle out of this verdict on the nuclear GRIMP by showing that the use of nuclear bombs may be a sensible choice and may not spell the end of civilization.

Henry Kissinger, in *Nuclear Weapons and Foreign Policy*, argued that a "limited nuclear war" is feasible. For instance, he wrote,

> In a limited war the problem is to apply graduated amounts of destruction for limited objectives and also to permit the necessary breathing spaces for political contacts.

I've already commented on such thinking in the preface of this book.

Herman Kahn, in *On Thermonuclear War*, went further, presenting a variety of scenarios including one with 100 million dead and, even so, stating that, "economic recuperation" will take just 100 years. In a scholarly approach he reasoned,

> *Objective studies indicate that even though the amount of human tragedy would be greatly increased in the postwar world, the increase would not preclude normal and happy lives for the majority of survivors and their descendents.*

Perhaps Kahn reasoned that because the world recovered from more than the 100 million deaths of World War II, we could survive a nuclear exchange. The analogy does not hold. After a nuclear exchange lasting a few minutes, not six years, the survivors, engulfed in a radioactive cloud, without food, would find their strength ebbing as they shoveled the debris — if they could even find a shovel.

In Civil Defense exercises of the 1950s, children practiced hiding under their school desks. Only decades later was it admitted that these drills were intended only to convince the leaders of the Soviet Union that we were crazy enough to participate in a nuclear exchange. Perhaps the Kissinger and Kahn books had the same goal, for anyone who thinks about the impact of nuclear bombs will quickly realize that once a nuclear exchange starts there may likely be no breathing space and that the survivors may not be so happy spending their lives burying the dead and searching for food. This particular GRIMP has lasted for over six decades.

As the years accumulate, confidence grows that the missiles with their nuclear warheads will never be launched in anger. However, back in 1962, the Cuban missile crisis put a dent in the graph of a rising sense of safety with this GRIMP. As the secretly recorded deliberations of President Kennedy and his advisers reveal, some thought much like Brodie, not like Kissinger and Kahn, for which we should be forever thankful.

Several times during those thirteen days of almost unbearable tension Kennedy spoke of the shadow that overhung all their give and take as they shaped a response to the Soviet missiles secretly deployed in Cuba. I quote just three of Kennedy's views of where one misstep could lead us and the world:

We could move very quickly into a world war over this, or to a nuclear war.

If we take out the missiles in a quick air strike, there's bound to be a reprisal, taking Berlin by force. Which leaves me only one alternative—and begin a nuclear exchange.

In extremis, everybody would use nuclear weapons. The decision to use any kind, even the tactical ones, presents such a risk of it getting out of control so quickly.

Luckily, the crisis passed, without the GRIMP ending in disaster. The Soviet Union agreed to remove its missiles; the United States promised, publicly, not to invade Cuba and, secretly, to remove its missiles from Turkey.

Since that peaceful resolution, faith that this GRIMP will never harm us has grown. No one knows how its graph will look in the long run, especially with the possibility of a terrorist acquiring a bomb.

In any case, this, the ultimate GRIMP, illustrates how we deal with any GRIMP. Make it as safe as we can. If possible, build it in stages. Live with it. Hope it does not end in disaster. Pay no attention to it. The uncertain arithmetic of a small number times a large leaves us only this risky approach.

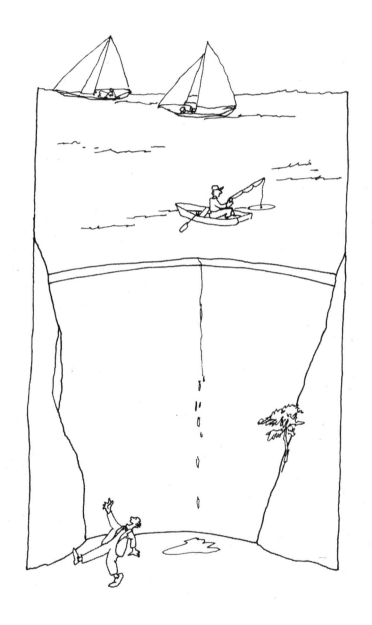

Does a GRIMP loom here?

18   What Is a Job?

The inevitable intruder; The two parts of a job;
The greatest invention.

Every month we can read the latest update on the number of
jobs created or lost. Jobs are important, especially if you don't
have one when you need it. So it is no surprise that the notion of a
job impinges on several chapters. Because worry about the loss or
creation of jobs can override the pros and cons of decisions, they
impinge on choice, especially the choice between incomparables.
Because we base our notion of expertise partly on our experience
in a job, jobs impinge on the coming chapters on expertise.

   Our notions about jobs shape our choices and can subvert
our ability to consider the pros and cons of issues.

THE INEVITABLE INTRUDER
That subversive force is suggested by these samples.

   · In a conflict about whether to permit a casino to open
   we have the headline, "Casino Means 2,800 Jobs."

   · When Magna Entertainment wanted to build a race-
   course in Dixon in the Sacramento Valley, it estimated that
   it would create 1,000 jobs at the facility and 2,000 at surrounding businesses. It pointed out that horse racing in

California was already a $4 billion industry, creating over 52,000 jobs. Residents of Dixon then had to weigh these benefits against impact on traffic and pollution.

· In opposition to an increase in the tobacco tax, this news item, "A study for the Tobacco Institute concluded that a 48-cent tax would eliminate 114,117 jobs."

· A frightening prediction of a loss of jobs was made when the National Do Not Call Registry was proposed. "It will be like an asteroid hitting the Earth," warned the telemarketing executive Tim Searcy: "Two million people will lose their jobs."

· The debate over revising the law concerning access to mineral deposits on public lands led to this warning: "Any significant change will lead to the loss of 50,000 jobs," with the reply, "All the jobs that may be lost can be made up by a single day of normal job growth."

· The decision whether to buy more supersonic stealth F-22 fighter planes focused not on their virtues and defects, but on the 90,000 jobs that would disappear if the contract were cancelled. Not by coincidence, those jobs were scattered through 44 states. No wonder 40 senators and 100 representatives pleaded to save this plane, which was designed in the 1980's to fight the Soviet Union. Spreading out the subcontractors was a triumph of what is called "political engineering."

It's easy to find examples in which conflict over the merits and demerits of a proposal is displaced by a battle of predictions concerning jobs lost or gained. In view of the wide concern over the number of jobs, we should think about the structure of what we traditionally call "a job."

This sounds like an academic exercise, but it is not. "What is water?" may seem a frivolous question too, but the discovery in the 18th century that water consists of hydrogen and oxygen helped inaugurate modern chemistry.

THE TWO PARTS OF A JOB

A job also is composed of two parts: a "production station" and an "income station." The production station describes what the worker does: repairs shoes, sells stocks, plays golf, or does nothing at all, perhaps inherits a fortune. The income station describes the money that the worker receives: millions of dollars in the case of a movie star or baseball player, much less for a teacher, or nothing whatsoever for a hospital volunteer. The income could even be negative, as it is for a museum docent, who not only serves free of charge, but even pays for the required training.

There is no law of economics that guarantees that the number of production stations automatically equals the number of income stations needed. It should come as no surprise, after all the mechanization and automation introduced over the last three centuries, that the essential tasks can be carried out by, say, two-thirds of the work force. The precise value of that fraction depends on the definition of "essential." It may be closer to one-half, for a survey of more than fifty management studies concluded that "American workers are actually working on producing for only about 55 percent of the time they are on the job." But taking its value as two-thirds, we may assume that one out of three workers is, from the production-station point of view, superfluous.

Only by sheer coincidence was there ever a balance between the supply of and demand for labor, as it was by chance that for centuries the size of the world population remained stable, the fertility rate matching the mortality rate. Just as science has upset that balance, it has upset the equally precarious balance between income stations and essential production stations.

While we may imagine that some invisible guiding hand assures an overall balance, we should be no more surprised than by seeing an imbalance in a small part of the economy. For instance, the number of violinists produced by conservatories far exceeds the demand, as anyone can confirm who has witnessed several hundred violinists show up at an audition to fill one vacancy.

One way to grasp the novelty of the new economics is to imagine that a giant machine spews out mountains of food, clothing, houses, and all the usual necessities and amenities. The machine, which produces enough for all, is run by a very small number of workers. This incredible cornucopia, this dream of mankind for ages, presents a new dilemma: How is everyone, including those not needed to run the machine, to share in its plenty? Economists call this the problem of distribution. As Jeremy Rifkin, president of the Foundation on Economic Trends, put it,

Every nation will have to grapple with the question of what to do with the millions of people whose labor is needed less, or not at all, in an ever-more-automated economy.

The fear of losing income stations can determine attitudes on even major issues. If jobs are threatened, concern over their disappearance can affect many deliberations. Moreover, since, by a historical quirk, health insurance is often tied to the job, having a job gains even more importance.

We usually model a job by thinking first of the production station. Then, as a secondary matter, we turn to the associated income station. But we get a more accurate model by thinking of a job first as an income station, with the actual work serving as a cover for the income. Clearly, a job, like those thirty lines in Chapter 1, *The Model*, can be viewed more than one way.

Such a perspective is not new. As far back as the Depression, when unemployment hovered at about a quarter of the work force, the government accepted the mission of increasing employment, through the creation of jobs by the Works Project Administration. That these jobs would supply goods and services was just a bonus.

But it was World War 2 that lifted the United States out of the depression. It became the "arsenal of democracy," producing incredible numbers of ships, planes, and tanks. This suggests that we can always invent income stations by creating an atmosphere of xenophobic fear. In such a mood, we could produce countless tanks, say, quickly declare them obsolete, and send them to the wrecking yards, thus creating even more jobs, both for those who build the tanks and for those who dismantle them.

The nonreturnable-container controversy quickly zeroed in on the fate of income stations. The industry predicted the loss of thousands of income stations in the manufacture of bottles. In arguing the case for recycling, Californians Against Waste responded that a returnable container system would result in "a net increase of 4,781 jobs."

In the Housing Act of 1937, the major concerns were unemployment and slum clearance. Provision of housing for the poor was only a peripheral goal. When seen in this light, the Pruitt Igoe housing development in Saint Louis, consisting of 32, 12-story buildings, which was demolished in 1974, was a major success. In *The Quality of Federal Policy Making: Programmed Failure in Public Housing,* Eugene Meehan observed that,

> *They were built at great cost, they lasted a very short time, and they were expensive to liquidate. In brief, they contributed more to the local economy in the short run than any other housing development in the city's history.*

It is odd that at the very moment that one part of society introduces labor-saving machines another part pushes labor-intensive tasks.

We have already created income stations by such means as earlier retirement and shorter workdays, as well as longer weekends, vacations, and lunch and coffee breaks. But this patchwork solution no longer suffices.

Economists evade the question of how much income should be assigned to a given production station. They defer to the law of supply and demand, as if that law is as consistently obeyed as Newton's law of gravitational attraction. They do not advocate that the income should be large enough to support the worker, nor do they put an upper limit on the income.

There is no ironclad relation between the value of the production station to society and its attached income; in any case, the occupant of a production station tries to expand the associated income by means fair or foul.

For instance, the Department of Transportation found in a survey of 62 automobile repair shops that 53 cents of each service dollar was wasted on needless repairs. The mechanics were doubling their income by such devices as offering a complete tune-up when only a new spark plug was needed. The California Bureau of Consumer Affairs conducted a similar study. Of 1300 vehicles with at least $2500 worth of "collision repairs," over 500 had parts or labor billed that were not actually supplied. The average overcharge was more than $800 per vehicle.

That is small potatoes when compared to the machinations of the heads of some large corporations. Even in a year where their companies lose money, they may walk off with bonuses larger than the yearly salaries of hundreds of their employees.

In Chapter 17, we met the general principle that a small number times a large one can be just about anything; in particular, the product can be large. This principle is exploited by mutual-fund managers, who charge about one percent of the value of the assets per year whether those assets rise or fall. That may explain why there are more than seven thousand mutual funds. The investors who pay that one percent fee are presumably in a position not to notice it and complain.

A municipal-bond counselor applies that "small times large can be large" principle also. The counselor's only responsibility is to rate the security behind a bond offering. Since that rating influences decisions by banks and the interest rate, it would be hoped that the counsel subjects each bond to a penetrating scrutiny requiring days or weeks. Such an assumption is unwarranted, as the dead-fish principle advises, and testimony in a Securities and Exchange Commission probe of New York City finances confirms:

Q: About how long does it take to prepare, to do the work and prepare an opinion?

A: Well, we have precedence in the office, so the actual time consumed is probably not more than an hour, considering preparation, typing and review.

The counsel should be praised for mastering the concept of the modern income station.

Only the naive or confused try to make money — that is, create an income station — in such arduous and indirect ways as growing food, making clothes, teaching children, or building shelters. To get water, you dip a pail directly into the river. The financial industry, with its brokers, underwriters, and rating agencies, applies this principle as it deals with the flow of astronomical sums of money. The bank robber applies the principle, but in a socially unacceptable manner.

So-called "paper entrepreneurs," usually trained in law, finance, or accounting, have mastered the principle. They arrange joint ventures and mergers, found holding companies, run mutual funds, and devise tax shelters. Their productive contributions may be obscure, but their income stations, placed near the rivers of money, are well-defined and large. No wonder that the financial sector of our economy grew to become larger than the manufacturing sector.

I am surprised that Senator Fitzgerald, in 2004, complained that the fee structure of the mutual fund industry is

> *the world's largest skimming operation — a $7 trillion trough from which fund managers, brokers and other insiders are steadily siphoning off an excessive slice of the nation's household, college and retirement savings.*

He simply overlooked the thousands of income stations supported by the generous skimming.

Because of the possible disparity between a production station and its associated income station, it is impolite to ask people how much they make. Even a law school professor, when studying law-firm incomes, ran into a brick wall. "We make an outrageous amount of money," he was told, "and we're not going to let it out." The secretive lawyer, clearly embarrassed by the disparity, was practicing the art of omission.

The economy that does not devise enough income stations attached to production stations creates a pressure to invent artificial income stations, either not connected to production stations or grossly inflated. These income stations take the form of larceny (grand and petty), scams, embezzlement, inflated bonuses, Ponzi schemes, arson and fake auto accidents for the insurance, and preposterous salaries. Such improvisations are so common that I once suggested to the *New York Times* that it run a column in its Sunday financial section to be called *Scams, Frauds, and Other Skullduggery.* They chose not to. Instead the front page of the financial news is full of headlines such as "Civil Charges are Expected in Fund Scandal," "Despite Lawsuit, Enron Bonuses Haven't Been Returned," "Health South's Former Chief is Expected to be Indicted." The frequency and the size of the scams make me wonder what fraction of the economy consists of ill-gotten gains. Yet one more research project for some economist.

THE GREATEST INVENTION

The modern unsung hero is the inventor of income stations. Demand an extra year of schooling, and presto, more income stations for teachers and a year's delay in millions of students' need for income stations. Or complicate the income tax forms and you make stations for accountants. The key is to agitate the economy, perhaps by a new invention or by an advertising campaign that creates fresh desires.

A baseball documentary set in the 1920s shows that almost every man in the stands was wearing a hat. By bringing hats back into fashion, you would create thousands of income stations.

Increased security, especially at airports, has created thousands of income stations without destroying any: the ideal innovation. The weight-loss industry should be praised for the same reason.

President Carter's plan to disallow the business lunch as a tax-deductible business expense foundered on concern for lost income stations. The National Restaurant Association estimated that if the business lunch were not tax deductible, 700,000 income stations in the restaurant and related industries would disappear. Carter evidently did not understand how enormous is the problem we face: We are trying to invent income stations while hiding this effort from our own eyes.

Disarmament would destroy income stations. Concern in 1972 that stopping the arms race would mean a perilous loss of income stations prompted Pope Paul VI to lament,

> *It is unthinkable that no work can be found for hundreds of thousands of workers other than the production of instruments of death.*

As though in response, the Sierra Club proposed an "environmental works program." It claimed that there were unfilled production stations, citing rehabilitation of decaying neighborhoods, park improvement, railroad track upkeep, home insulation, restoration of grazing land, and control of erosion — all culled from the backlog of unfunded government projects. (I add fixing the potholes in Highway 80 or providing a second track so the southbound train from Seattle to Los Angeles doesn't have to be moved to a siding to allow the northbound train to pass.) The contrast between the Pope's plea and the Sierra Club's response takes us back to the chapter on the implicit choice.

During the recession that started in 2008 we consumers were asked to go out and buy in order to rescue the economy and create jobs. That is an odd request, given that the economy is there to serve us. The economy should reflect our needs. If some guru persuaded us to shed our possessions and live simply, the economy would collapse, and the preservation of jobs would become a crucial issue.

Perhaps the Department of Labor should be renamed, just as the Department of War became the Department of Defense. It should be called the Department of Production and Income Stations. The new name would remind us of the possible imbalance between the two types. The Department would have the task of maintaining an equilibrium between the available production stations and the workers seeking income stations. If we disregard the need to balance them, the issue of jobs lost or gained will continue to drown out what would otherwise be the main concerns in resolving many issues.

EXPERTS

19 The Two Types of Experts

The professional and the shaman;
Even we need shamans.

Now that I have dealt with the theme of "jobs," which intrudes into our thinking especially when there are not enough of them, I will explore how we cope with the challenges described in the earlier chapters. In order to deal with difficult decisions, we single out certain individuals as especially wise, possessing more reliable models, more adept in choosing between incomparables, and more skilled in the art of prediction. These chosen ones we call "experts."

An expert, presumed to possess a greater degree of skill or knowledge in some area, is more highly developed than we run-of-the-mill mortals, who are called "layperson," "average Joe," or "outsider." By contrast, "expert," in its widest sense, refers to anyone who through office, experience, training, or celebrity carries more weight than a layperson.

An expert may be identified by title, such as "President," by specialty, such as "economist," " psychologist," or "juggler," or by status, such as "insider," "consultant," "pundit," or "authority." In some cases, expertise may be indicated by a degree or uniform, as in the case of a doctor or general.

For us to feel secure we must believe that the forces shaping our lives are under control. The creation and preservation of this belief has been the responsibility of certain individuals in cultures throughout the world. This role also falls upon the experts in our society that has released new demons of its own. Our experts have two distinct functions: to control events and to convey the illusion that they control events.

THE PROFESSIONAL AND THE SHAMAN

Those two functions require different types of experts.

The first type demands assured competence in a particular field. We call such experts "professionals." That is one of the definitions you will find in a dictionary. Another is "one engaged in a specific activity as a source of livelihood." Sociologists define a professional indirectly. First they define a profession as a group that can license and control its work, as granted by society. (The medical profession is a prime example.) The members of this group are then called professionals. In practice my definition overlaps that one, but it's not the same. According to mine, a professional need not belong to an officially recognized group. Nor need my professionals earn their livelihoods from their work.

The juggler is the archetype of what I call a professional. He describes precisely what he will do, then does it, and there is no doubt that he has done it. When he simultaneously keeps three bowling pins spinning in the air, balances a ball on his nose, and twirls a hoop while riding a unicycle, we can judge his accomplishment immediately.

Since his performance is isolated from the flow of the world's events, our evaluation is not plagued with quibbles like "on the other hand," "what if," "it's too soon to tell," "he couldn't have foreseen such and such." The single object of his performance is to earn instantaneous appreciation. The utter uselessness of his task helps the juggler focus our attention on the brilliance of its execution.

Part of the pleasure in watching professional sports may be seeing expertise demonstrated before one's very eyes: the second baseman, while leaping over a plunging runner, throws to first base; the quarterback, evading certain tackles, gets off a perfect pass to a receiver guarded by three defenders; the basketball player scores from 3-point range without the ball even touching the rim.

At the very opposite of the professional, as symbolized by the juggler, stand those experts, such as psychiatrists, whose skills are difficult to confirm. To evaluate them we must resort to inspecting secondary characteristics, just as we sometimes determine the sex of a bird by the color of its feathers. We may judge psychiatrists by their years of experience or by the decor of their waiting rooms. It is much harder to know that the psychiatrist has healed a soul than whether a ball is balancing on the juggler's nose. If the soul is not healed, who is to blame? The patient, the psychiatrist, or a mad society? And if it is healed, who should get the credit? Perhaps time alone did the trick — who knows?

But psychiatrists have a second task: by their existence, to reassure the public by the trappings of expertise that the demons are under control.

EVEN WE NEED SHAMANS

Each society has to develop its own rituals for dealing with those forces of man and nature that it cannot control. Prayers, sacred songs, dances to the gods, and sacrifices helped primitive tribes contend with calamity and the unknown. It may not have been the main purpose of the rain dance to produce rain. The deeper purpose may have been to induce in the tribe the feeling it was in control of its destiny. Who could face the stark model of a universe in which rain and drought alternated at random, indifferent to man's needs? Perhaps not all members of the tribe had equal access to supernatural powers. In that case, an individual recognized to have special access was appointed to contact the evil or the good spirits. This shaman, or witch doctor, enabled a society to sustain its sense of order.

This definition of a shaman may be more general than the one anthropologists use. Even so, I will stick with mine. I do not mean to offend those who have studied shamans. I was even tempted to make "shaman" singular and use "shamen" for the plural. But I have already stepped on enough toes without also disturbing learned grammarians who try to protect the English language from gratuitous change.

The archetypal shaman in our world is the astrologist, who offers clients the illusion of insight into the future. Astrologists can still make a good living, casting horoscopes nowadays using computers. The traditional justification for the importance of these horoscopes is that, "since the sun obviously impacts our lives, so must the planets." Yet, as far back as the year 397, Saint Augustine in his *Confessions* devoted several pages to show that astrology was nonsense. He described an "experiment" carefully conducted by the father of a friend: "The two women gave birth simultaneously, forcing them to assign exactly the same horoscope, even in the finest detail, to both babies, the one to his son, the other to his slave... Yet [his friend] pursued quite a brilliant career ... while the slave-boy went on serving his masters." That astrology flourishes sixteen centuries later speaks to our hunger to have a sense of control over the future.

In that delightful 1940 exposé of Wall Street, *Where Are the Customers' Yachts,* the Wall Street insider, Fred Schwed Jr. offered a clear contrast of the professional and the shaman. He asked rhetorically wouldn't you want to put our savings in a mutual fund [then called an 'investment trust'] run by an expert? Wouldn't you want the best golfer, Mr. Sarazen, to make your shots for you? Then he answered his questions.

> *This would be an airtight analogy, except for one thing, Mr. Sarazen is superior to you and me at playing golf, and he can demonstrate this superiority every time he steps on the first tee. But thus far in our history there has been little evidence that there exists a demonstrable skill in managing security portfolios.*

His remark remains valid today, with Sarazen replaced by Tiger Woods.

It is debatable whether shamans of tribes more primitive than ours have supernatural powers. But an anthropological study of a Mexican Indian tribe did show shamans think differently from non-shamans. When confronted with a blurred photograph and asked, "What is it?," shamans were much less likely to reply, "I don't know." Moreover, shamans are much more likely to impose their own interpretation and to disregard suggestions. Anthropologists call this being "inner directed." Shamans are more likely to depend on their own world models and to be less open to new facts from the outer world. They share some characteristics with the garrulous psychics we will meet in Chapter 25.

We assign the role of the shaman in our own society to certain experts, authorities or high officials, whose very presence assures us that someone is in charge, that someone is contending with the problems that plague us, whether inflation, recession, unemployment, pollution, energy, or terrorism. We don't think they have supernatural powers, only that they are wiser or at least know something we do not.

But they may not be wiser and they may not know more than we do. As Senator Byrd warned us in Losing America, we believe,

> *that members of Congress know a lot more than the average American when it comes to secret information. The plain truth is we know more, but not a great deal more. Especially when classified information pertains to controversial presidential adventures, we get as much or as little as may suit the White House ... Secrecy ... keeps prying eyes from criticizing.*

So even our elected representatives can be victims of distortion by omission, rendering them as helpless as we.

Our shamans do not wear animal masks and feathers or approach the spirits through chants, trances, and the ringing of hand bells. The rituals of the shaman vary from tribe to tribe, and in particular for the tribes that inhabit the developed world.

Our shamans speak well. They don't sprinkle their sentences with "uh," "er," "I mean," and "you know." They have an impressive vocabulary, a jargon replete with technical terms that imply expertise. Their sentences flow. They can speak in whole paragraphs. Some can talk so rapidly that it is hard to tell whether they are discussing the present or the future. The deeper their voice, the more convincing they become. The one trait I have noticed that financial advisers share is not that they give good advice or can see into the future. Rather, they are all persuasive.

We should not smugly assume that we are above the need of shamans. On the contrary, our great problems, which we seem unable to solve, require their services. In another society, shamans may cast a spell at the time of plowing, sowing, and harvesting. Our shamans offer incantations to assure us all will go well with a campaign to solve the problem of crime, or revenue from a new subway will cover expense, or a trillion dollar bailout will solve an economic crisis, or a preventive war will be short and welcomed by the invaded. They can be counted on to bless the start of a Grimp. We think of them as wiser than we, but as John Galbraith wrote in *The Great Crash of 1929,*

> *Wisdom is often an abstraction associated not with fact or reality, but with the man who asserts it and the manner of its assertion.*

When a mad cow is discovered to have entered the food chain we are comforted by a front-page article with the headline, "Experts Try to Assess Risk From Diseased Cow." Even though the word "try" may alarm us, we are relieved that we don't have to become vegetarians.

Shamans are called upon to predict the effect of a reduction in federal taxes. Endorsing the cut in 2003, a supply-side economist assured our tribe the cut would easily produce the promised one million new jobs, "This is the most pro-growth tax cut we've seen since 1981." But another economist foresaw that "over the next decade it would cost jobs, in part, because the resulting rise in budget deficits would push interest rates higher."

Since jobs are constantly being created and lost, even without manipulation of the tax code, we may never know who is right. The gain or loss due to the tax cut may not be noticed in the larger common fluctuations of an economy with over 140,000,000 non-farm jobs. Besides, the nation itself is not static, for it grows by 3,000,000 people a year. No wonder it is nearly impossible for an economist to confirm or refute a theory by experiments the way a physicist or chemist can. While politicians delight in promising that tax cuts expand the economy, economists have been unable to justify that claim.

An expert may be part professional and part shaman, able to exercise skills of control as well as to convey an illusion of control. A physicist is a professional when discussing atomic energy, but is a shaman when asserting in a choice between incomparables that the need for energy more than balances the risks in its production. The Navajo shaman practiced both forms of expertise. He located lost objects, diagnosed serious diseases, assisted in difficult childbirths, and predicted the outcome of a war raid. He helped control events by practicing a professional skill, but he also helped create the illusion of control, so essential at the start of a fresh enterprise. In our society the shamans who perform this second role are not easily identified, for, to achieve their effect, they must conceal their true role behind the mask of professional expertise. We laypersons must be able to say to ourselves, "They know something that we don't."

It is in our own interest to be able to distinguish between the professional and the shaman. Chapter 21 presents a few rules of thumb that have helped me tell them apart. But the next chapter shows one reason it is hard to tell them apart.

20 Expert Creep

Expert creep, good and bad;
The president as shaman.

When I contrasted the professional and the shaman, I noted the same person can play both roles, just as Pooh-Bah in Gilbert and Sullivan's *Mikado* shifts from one role to another without any change in appearance. If we are not alert, we may not notice the shift from professional to shaman. One moment we see before us the well-credentialed professional, a clear-cut expert in a field. Then, poof, the next moment he has turned into a shaman speaking about a subject of which he knows no more than the audience does. The shift is as hard to detect as a magician's sleight-of-hand.

The magician depends on the hand being faster than the eye. What I call "expert-creep," the professional transformed into a shaman, depends instead on events happening faster than the mind can process them. To spot expert-creep we must stay alert, for this switch is more common than we may suspect.

Friends suggested that I call it "expert-shift" to give it a neutral tone. I later found out that writers on critical thinking call it "authority borrowing." However, "expert-creep" serves as more of a warning, just as the "dead-fish principle" is more alarming than the "billboard principle."

EXPERT-CREEP: GOOD AND BAD

Expert-creep is neither good nor bad. It all depends on how it is used. In a democracy, where we are all encouraged to participate in settling conflicts, expert-creep is inevitable.

William Shockley, winner of the Nobel Prize in Physics in 1956 for the invention of the transistor, exploited his fame to help propagate his belief that intellectual capacity varied from race to race, a proposition discredited by psychologists and geneticists.

Albert Einstein also took on the role of the shaman. A professional as a physicist discussing the theory of relativity, he spoke out on many of the world's problems that had nothing to do with physics. For instance, he advised, "We must be prepared to make the same heroic sacrifices for the cause of peace that we make ungrudgingly for the cause of war."   His expertise in physics allowed him to practice as a shaman in many areas.

Why did people pay attention to him as a shaman? Why did his words carry more weight than those of the person-in-the-street or the next-door neighbor? Perhaps it was sheer awe. Or perhaps the listener subconsciously felt, "Since he thinks so deeply about the physical world, he must also think deeply about the human world," or, "If he said something untrue, he would look foolish. He would not risk blemishing his reputation, for he has too much to lose." Or, "He must circulate with others as wise as he, not with ordinary mortals, so he knows more than I about everything."

Einstein knew he was exploiting his fame as a scientist to shape events outside his area of expertise. When John Kemeny, later to serve as president of Dartmouth, came to him with a fresh Ph.D. in mathematics to be his assistant, he asked Einstein for advice. Kemeny said he wanted to do good in the world, even if that meant leaving mathematics. Einstein told him that in order to do good, he should first establish a reputation as a mathematician; that would provide a way to do good in other areas. Kemeny took his advice.

As I mentioned in Chapter 10, Bishop Berkeley anticipated Einstein in this observation, but warned the layperson to be on guard against expert-creep. Though I am a mathematician, I cannot be accused of practicing expert-creep in writing this book. Perhaps

I am practicing the opposite of expert-creep, showing that mathematics and numbers have limited use in settling real-world issues.

We witness a common form of expert-creep when George Foreman, a retired boxer, appears in ads for automobile mufflers or culinary grills. This is just one example of assigning expertise to a "celebrity," someone who has achieved name recognition without committing an outrageous crime.

Perhaps the first use of celebrities to sell something not related to their expertise was having Charlie Chaplin stump for war bonds during World War I. If he was for them, they must be a good idea. In a sense, Charlie certified that investing in a bond would be not only patriotic but safe. A celebrity surely would not want to endorse a shoddy product. This test is "proof by celebrity" or "innocence by association," another technique alien to mathematicians — an intensely self-reliant gang who resist "proof by authority figure."

As we look back over our presidents, we see perhaps the ultimate in expert-creep. The president of the United States must face so diverse an array of decisions about matters domestic and foreign that no particular training or experience — whether in law, psychology, management, business, political science — could possibly certify someone as being prepared to bear the awesome responsibilities of that office.

While sitting in a doctor's waiting room, we draw comfort from the diplomas on the wall, which assure us the person on the other side of the door is qualified to practice medicine. I can imagine no analogous certificate, no matter how ornate the lettering, that would assure that so-and-so has the necessary prerequisites to practice the presidency.

THE PRESIDENT AS SHAMAN

The leap from any office to the office of President is so great that it's hard to imagine any preparation is adequate. As we review in our minds the lives of Presidents, we find victorious generals, senators, representatives, and governors. They all possessed name recognition and had experience in being part of an organization.

But think of the preparation of any one of them, say, Jimmy Carter: officer on a nuclear submarine, peanut farmer, governor of a small state, Sunday school teacher. Or George W. Bush, oilman, baseball entrepreneur, governor of a large state where the governor has little power.

No one dares think or say, "I am qualified to be President." Instead, the thought must be, "No one is better qualified, so I may as well seek the office." Jimmy Carter thought of running for President after getting a close look at announced candidates while ferrying them around Georgia.

A candidate must address certain issues, but the voter realizes that those may well not be the ones the candidate will face in the four long years of a presidential term. So the voter is obliged to judge the candidate as a person, by reviewing the record, noting effectiveness before a microphone, and observing how well the campaign runs. These are secondary signs of expertise for a President, as they must be. While Harry Truman once said that a President must be one-quarter actor, the President is much more a shaman.

We can hope the expertise of the general or senator or governor somehow transfers to the presidency, but all we may settle for is an aura of leadership. No wonder the taller candidate and the one who more deftly transforms the complex into simple emotional tidbits tend to be elected.

We need both types of experts, but we should not pretend a shaman is a professional. We must, out of our own self-interest, be on the watch for expert-creep.

21 How to Tell a Shaman from a Professional

How to spot a professional;
How to spot a shaman.

Just as it is prudent of us to distinguish whether on a particular issue we are wise or foolish, it is advisable to be able to tell the shaman from a professional.

While among the experts in our society some are pure professionals and others pure shamans, many experts perform both roles in varying degrees, but without indicating, say, by a change of costume, which one they are playing. They may not even notice the shift themselves, a failing which makes it even more difficult for us to spot the shift. A few rules of thumb help distinguish between the two types.

HOW TO SPOT A PROFESSIONAL

The professional tends to be concerned with well-defined tasks usually in the physical realm, set in the present, not controversial, repeatable, and easy to evaluate. The bypass-surgeon, the plumber, and the bridge designer are typical examples. By contrast, the shaman more likely deals with ill-defined tasks, stretching into the future, controversial, involving choice, and hard to evaluate. Typical is the economist contending with recession, inflation, and unemployment,

The professional works within the framework of a well-defined state-of-the-art, reflected in a training that culminates in the award of a generally accepted certificate of completion. Elaborate handbooks and regulations based on experience and experiment define performance standards in the field.

The shaman works in a field where the state of the art is ill-defined and seems to remain in perpetual infancy because its assumptions cannot be tested by experiment. Thus, in a trial where experts testify on both sides we may suspect the presence of shamans. This definition of an expert some wag once made applies to shamans: "We may define experts as people who can authentically disagree with each other."

The performance of the professional can be evaluated directly. It is fairly easy to determine whether a bridge stands or a faucet leaks. The possibility of such an audit is the most telling criterion separating professional from shaman. The shaman's performance, partly because it may not be completed for decades, partly because it is woven into a larger fabric whose design is out of his control, may be impossible to monitor while in progress, or to audit upon completion.

HOW TO SPOT A SHAMAN

The professional is seldom seen in public. However, the need to convince the public that some great new project, especially a GRIMP, will succeed calls for the display of shamans. A press conference or bank of microphones is the clearest sign in our tribe of the presence of a shaman. A shaman can be counted on always to testify on the same side of an issue, this being viewed as a sign of consistency rather than of bias. One economic shaman will always testify in favor of less government interference, whatever the issue; another will predictably favor government intervention.

The layperson must remember that the expert as shaman may, when the heat of confrontation passes, revert to the role of expert as professional. Just as a person may one moment be a pedestrian and the next a driver, an expert can shift from one phase to the other.

Professionals are identified by their accomplishments. This simply reflects the comparative ease of the audit. Secondary characteristics, such as title or uniform, serve merely to facilitate the performance of the task. The reverse holds in the case of the shaman. The more diffuse the task, the more ambiguous and time-consuming the audit, the more must shamans be judged by symbol rather than by substance. The expertise of the shaman may be suggested by such signs as a special prefix or suffix attached to the name, an ornate office or magnificent desk, a signed photograph of the expert shaking hands with a more famous expert, or special dignity-enhancing robes.

Our shamans are like the witch doctors of Zaire, who adopt certain mannerisms to separate themselves from laypersons – special ways to dress and speak, even a special name when they work.

To test our understanding of the distinction between shaman and professional, consider this report to Congress of Ben Bernanke, head of the Federal Reserve:

> *If actions taken by the Administration, the Congress, and the Federal Reserve are successful in restoring some measure of financial stability — and only if that is the case, in my view — there is a reasonable prospect that the current recession will end in 2009 and that 2010 will be a year of recovery.*

What does "some measure of financial stability" mean? What does "reasonable prospect" mean? How will we know that the recession is over? The fuzziness that permeates the report shows that Bernanke was acting as shaman. Further evidence is that other economists were claiming that the steps taken were too small, others, too large, and some that lowering taxes was the better way. Besides, we will never be sure what role, if any, the various efforts played in the eventual recovery.

This is not to criticize Bernanke, who works in a field that by its nature must turn its brightest practitioners into shamans, especially when facing the perfect storm of excess credit, fraud, subprime mortgages, poorly managed automobile manufacturers, shrinking newspapers, excess faith in mathematical formulas to evaluate risk, inadequate regulation, and excess leverage that combined to bring liquidity to a halt. Rather, it is to illustrate how to spot a shaman.

Next, let us go one step further, testing our understanding both of shamans and the dead-fish principle, the "put-your-best-foot-forward" principle. We will inspect a full-page advertisement of a brokerage firm, which appeared in the *New York Times* January 27, 2004.

The ad begins with a question set in letters half an inch high and occupies a third of the page: "Looking for a mutual fund with strong performance?" It goes on, in letters just as high, "This is where we come in."

There are already the twin implications that the firm's funds have done well in the past and that, consequently, you can expect them to do well in the future, because they are run by experts.

Let us look at one of the eight funds described, whose performance was typical of the other seven. In the preceding year, 2003, it grew by 38.55%, which is impressive. Giving it to so many significant digits is more impressive than saying simply 39%. The ad also lists the average annual growth in the last five years, a mere 2.68%. That sends off alarm bells. That the average growth was so small in spite of the phenomenal growth in 2003 should make us wonder what the average growth was during the first four years.

A little arithmetic done on a hand calculator shows that for those four years on the average the fund lost 4.73% annually. That would not cheer the potential investor.

As we continue to practice the dead-fish principle, we read the print below the table that shows all the growth numbers. Here the letters are only one-sixteenth of an inch high. The fine print says,

> *Past performance is no guarantee of future results...*
> *Value will fluctuate and shares, when redeemed, may*
> *be worth more or less than their original cost.*

Now we are perplexed: Does past performance imply anything about the future? If not, then why publish the table showing past performance? The skilled "dead-fisher" or "best-footer" would have read the fine print first and no further, and smile with admiration of the shamans who, making no promise whatsoever, earn their fee no matter what happens to the value of a share.

Year after year some column in the financial pages reminds potential investors that if they simply put their money in a non-managed fund that is indexed to Standard and Poor's list of five hundred stocks, they will do as well as or better than by following the advice of their broker. Even so, brokers thrive.

Unfortunately for our tribe, the more important and novel the challenge for which we call upon the service of an expert, the more likely it is that the expert will serve as shaman rather than as professional. For this reason it is critical that we learn to tell the two types apart. With practice, anyone can become an expert in making the critical distinction and in spotting expert-creep even in its subtlest form.

However, some projects, such as improving education, rescuing the economy, reducing poverty, or invading and rebuilding another nation, are so full of uncertainty that they become great equalizers, turning professionals into shamans, shamans into outsiders, and outsiders into shamans and even into professionals.

22 The Shaman–Layman Contract

The fine print; Our three impulses.

Shamans derive their authority from the accomplishments of professionals, from their own charisma, and from the needs and credulity of us outsiders. It is in the mutual interest of our shamans and us to cultivate faith in the expertise of the shamans. We can then shift to the shamans the burden of unpleasant choices. Moreover, they can then speak more dogmatically than is justified by the facts.

Experts, whether professional or shaman, are granted the right to offer conclusory statements, that is, to state opinions without showing how they reached them. Thus the expert has the same right in the public arena that the expert witness enjoys in the courtroom. An expert can say, "The United States is now in the most vulnerable condition in its history," and we tremble; a layperson who makes such a claim would not even be heard. We outsiders are free to believe the shaman has inside information not generally available.

Just as a number carries more weight than a word, so the pronouncement of an expert casts over us a spell that an outsider can rarely duplicate. This effect can be achieved in any field, as we can verify by our reactions to such varied headlines as "Expert says sculpture is not beyond saving," "Experts fear slower growth rate," and "Experts predict need for nuclear energy." A letter to the editor carries much more weight when the writer is identified as being part of an organization; this lifts the writer above the status of mere layperson.

THE FINE PRINT

To perpetuate the illusion of superior wisdom on the part of the expert requires tacit cooperation between shamans and the public. We laypersons agree not to audit the performance of the shamans; instead, we tolerate a wide margin of error.

Thus Cyrus Vance, who had served as a high official during the Vietnam War, could admit with impunity at the hearings for his confirmation as Secretary of State,

> Let me say, in light of hindsight, it was a mistake to intervene in Vietnam. I knew I made more than my share of mistakes. We learned a number of lessons in Vietnam and I'm wiser for that.

It is better to be wrong gracefully than right bluntly. After all, there was no attempt to find a critic of the Vietnam War, someone who had been right from the beginning, to serve as Secretary of State. That is not the way things are done. No one proposed O. Edmund Clubb, who, in *Trap in Vietnam*, published in 1962, foresaw the ultimate failure of American intervention:

> The American hypothesis is based upon a failure to appreciate the very essence of guerilla warfare. If France put 200,000 men into its eight-year Indo-China war and lost, might we not have to, over a decade if required, put in 500,000 men?

His figure was almost right on the button, but such insight has little to do with the role of shaman.

Since we do not expect perfection from shamans, President Carter, who occupied what could be called the office of chief shaman, could confess,

It's impossible for anyone to anticipate all future political events. And I think that the rapid change of affairs in Iran has not been predicted by anyone so far as I know.

Therefore it was in poor taste for *The Nation* to cite the timely warnings that had appeared in its columns, such as, "The Shah of Iran's authoritarian dynasty appears to be disintegrating," November, 1978, two months before the collapse, and, "The small, spontaneous demonstrations that broke out in isolated spots around Iran a year ago have coalesced into a massive resistance movement encompassing virtually every sector of the society," October, 1978. But similar alarms had been sounded in the magazine long before, such as this one in March, 1961, "Riots have broken out in Teheran ... Time is running out on the Shah." Time was indeed running out, but water can hiss a long time before it boils. Carter may be forgiven for not heeding the warnings.

A tribe that habitually rebuffs its shamans may lose respect for higher authority. A rug importer went too far, "I bought heavily in Iran just before the fall of the Shah," which he had anticipated. "So did everybody else. Only Jimmy Carter was caught with his pants down." His pants down? A tribe cannot long treat its shamans with such disrespect and still keep the proper distance between shaman and layperson.

OUR THREE IMPULSES

We outsiders have three conflicting impulses. One is to deify shamans, to endow them with mysterious powers of insight and foresight. The second is to show that they are just ordinary persons, hence a preoccupation with our leaders' private lives. The third is to topple our leaders, to remind them that those who lifted them high can bring them low as well. The very ropes with which we raise the statue can be used to pull it down.

The shaman must be above us and yet of us, the offspring of a god and a mortal, such as appear in several religions. It is the obligation of the shaman to preserve this appearance, to emulate that king who, according to Herodotus,

I allowed no one to have direct access to his person, but made all communication pass through the hands of

*messengers. He feared that his peers, if they saw him
frequently, would be pained at the sight and would therefore be likely to conspire against him; whereas if they
did not see him, they would think him quite a different
sort of being from themselves.*

The shamans of today have a similar fear. When the Library of
Congress released Justice Thurgood Marshall's papers — drafts,
working papers, churlish asides — the Supreme Court was upset.
Professor Hutchinson of the University of Chicago Law School
explained its reaction,

*The Court's afraid of being demystified. The myth of rea-
soned detachment is one the Court clings to ferociously.
They're afraid it's the myth or nothing, that they'll be
seen as either apostles of principled deliberation or as
scoundrels.*

That may be why they have resisted TV in their courtroom for
years after both houses of Congress accepted it. We laypersons
must agree with the Court, for we make little effort to discover
what transpires in its inner sanctum. In particular, we do not want
to find out what each of the nine justices thought as they chose
the victor in the presidential election of 2000.

In the time of a natural or manmade disaster, such as the
collapse of a GRIMP, the shaman will be able to draw upon this
divine capital, as does a governor who flies over a flood or a president who visits the site of the World Trade Center soon after its
destruction. Such actions reassure us that all will be well and we
can go back to our daily affairs.

Just as it is not in the layperson's interest to deflate the
shaman, it is certainly not in the interest of the shaman to reveal
that the evil spirits are beyond his control. It was unwise for the
Nuclear Regulatory Commission to tape its private deliberations
during the Three Mile Island crisis in 1979 and foolish to publish
them verbatim when they contained such confessions as,

*We are operating almost totally in the blind. His infor-
mation is ambiguous, mine is non-existent and — I don't
know — it's like a couple of blind men staggering around
making decisions,"* and *" It is a failure mode that has*

never been studied. It is just unbelievable. No plant has ever been in this condition, no plant has ever been tested in this condition, no plant has ever been analyzed in this condition in the history of this program.

A society that demands ever more complex technological as well as economic and social programs depends on shamans to assert they will work as planned. It cannot tolerate experts who reveal they cannot control the demons. It would have been better if the tapes made of the White House deliberations during the Cuban missile crisis had been destroyed, for they reveal how great was the risk of a nuclear war. On the other hand, since the crisis ended peacefully, we are free to find reassurance in that the ultimate GRIMP did not get out of control, thus providing a neat illustration of the perceptual option.

It is unfortunate when an expert, perhaps a shaman himself, exposes the behind-the-scenes truth that some shamans are just glorified laypersons, though usually more articulate than the typical person in the street. The advice Peter Eldin gave to magicians in *The Magic Handbook* applies to shamans:

Never tell anyone how the tricks are done. The basic appeal is that the audience does not know how your miracles are accomplished. As soon as you tell someone the secret, you destroy the illusion that you are a great magician.

Luckily, few people read the economist Paul Ormerod's introduction to his book, *The Death of Economics*, where he confessed,

Its practitioners pronounce with great confidence in the media, and have created around the discipline a barrier of jargon and mathematics, which have made the subject difficult to penetrate for the non-initiated.

Orthodox economics is in many ways an empty box. The basis is deeply flawed. Good economists know, from work carried out in their own discipline, that the foundations of their subject are virtually non-existent.

He is not the only economist to question the foundation of his profession. James K. Galbraith lamented the failure of almost all economists to foresee the recession of 2008,

> *It's an enormous blot on the reputation of our profession. There are thousands of economists. Most of them teach. And most of them teach a theoretical framework that has been shown to be fundamentally useless.*

This jibes with my own observations. For years economists offered as an axiom, as precise as an axiom in mathematics, that inflation and high unemployment cannot occur together. When the axiom was violated in the 1970s, they invented a new word, "stagflation."

Once we acknowledge the limits of economics, we will have a harder time treating the predictions of economists as seriously as we would like. In that case, we will have to accommodate ourselves to living with a bit more uncertainty, which illustrates why we outsiders happily continue to abide by that unwritten contract between the shamans and ourselves. We do not want to upset a happy equilibrium.

AUDIT AND PROPHECY

23   The Audit: Did It Work?

Did it work? Don't expose our shamans.

For a professional the audit is fairly straightforward, but the audit of a shaman is marked by ambiguity and unavoidable delays. It's not the way things are in mathematics, where a proof of a new theorem can be checked word for word, step by step. Nor is it like the practice in science, where you can repeat experiments done in other laboratories. In the real world there is seldom a chance to repeat an experiment. Besides, the principals themselves may not want an audit, and outsiders, having enough on their minds, may say, "What's done is done." A few examples will show what I mean.

DID IT WORK?

President Johnson in 1967 announced:

> *I have sent today to the Congress the Safe Streets and Crime Control Act. It calls for the most comprehensive attack on crime ever undertaken. The Federal Government can help train better police forces and give them modern equipment — to stem the rising tide of organized crime, to stop the illegal flow of narcotics, and to keep lethal weapons out of the wrong hands.*

Backing this Act of great promise was the advice of social scientists and criminologists. The legislators supported it with $4 billion through 1975, without, however, the desired result of making streets safe or controlling crime. Although the crime rate rose, experts could reply that it would have risen more without the Act. We are left comparing the real world with a world that might have been, and comparing this use of the money with implicit alternatives. A former administrator explained later, "It was not designed for nor is it capable of directly reducing crime."

The first obstacle to monitoring an action is that its goal is so ill defined that it is hard to tell whether it has been met.

A second obstacle is that a complex program can result in a mixture of failure and success. The more it improves one part, say the police, the more inefficient another part may become, say the overburdened courts.   An audit requires simultaneous comparisons on several scales. Once again we face the problem of comparing incomparables.

Third, the public is little concerned with the waste of vast amounts of money. There is usually no dramatic occasion to look back and take stock. The start of a government program, like a wedding, is marked by fanfare, but its end, like a divorce, passes with little notice. It is not in the interest of the experts involved to criticize the program. Other experts will shy away from conducting an audit, in part because they would appear to be spoilsports, and in part because they would not want to prejudice the audits of their own projects.

When the program is left unjudged, the experts who created it are not judged either. The public, so alert to bargains at garage sales, shows no concern at the disappearance of $4 billion. After all, that money was not shredded and dropped as confetti on a Fifth Avenue parade. As in a lottery, it was moved around, with a few benefiting handsomely and with many painlessly losing a little.

The start of an enterprise is accompanied by detailed studies, impact statements, and the predictions of experts. A retrospective look is either absent or at best anecdotal. The comments of Arundhati Roy in *Shall We Learn from the Experts* on the big dams in India apply, with the change of a few words, to countless undertakings:

> *Isn't it odd that there is no reliable estimate of how many people have been displaced? That there is no estimate for exactly what the contributions of big dams have been to overall food production? That there hasn't been an official audit, a post-project evaluation of a single big dam to see whether it has achieved what it set out to achieve? Whether the costs were justified, or even what the costs actually were?*

It may be easier to judge the success of a dam than of the Safe Streets Act, but it wouldn't be simple. The auditor would have to compare such incomparables as the increase in food production against the loss of community ties. Moreover the auditor would have to make long-term predictions, such as how soon the dam will silt up. For a thorough evaluation, the auditor would also look back at the predictions of both the supporters and the opponents of the project. Finally, different auditors may reach different conclusions.

In their book, *Megaprojects and Risk,* Flyvbjerg, Bruzelius, and Rothengatter lament the absence of audits of large-scale enterprises.

> *Given the large amounts of money spent... it is remarkable how little data and research are available that would help answer the two basic questions: "Whether such projects have the intended effects?" and "How the actual viability of such projects compares to projected viability?"*

Auditing a GRIMP presents quite a challenge. If the feared disaster has not occurred, then all is rosy. If it does occur, then all that is left to do is run a postmortem to try to discover how it happened, as in Bhopal, the Teton dam, or Chernobyl.

A RUTHLESS AUDIT

One of the harshest audits, written by the expert himself, appeared in *In Retrospect*, in which Robert McNamara looked back on his performance as Secretary of Defense during the Vietnam War. The book, which appeared a quarter century after the war, reads like a confession of numerous sins of omission, of which the following three are a small sample:

> *I clearly erred by not coercing a knock-down drag-out debate over loose assumptions, unasked questions, and their analyses.*

> *Could I have handled the issues with greater effort in shortening the war? I could have and should have.*

> *I misunderstood the nature of the conflict.*

McNamara was brave to confess publicly, and prudent to wait a decent interval to do so. Even so, this self-audit omitted sins of commission, of which there was at least one. When he and Daniel Ellsberg were returning from an inspection tour in Vietnam, McNamara asked Ellsberg what he thought about our progress. Ellsberg replied that things were the same as the previous year. McNamara then suggested that, because we had increased our forces, it meant the situation was worse than a year before. Ellsberg agreed. However, when they landed, McNamara told the reporters,

> *I'm glad to be able to tell you that we're making great progress in every dimension of our effort.*

In this deception he was playing a part in the effort to mislead the American people, as recounted in detail in Ellsberg's book, *Secrets*. It is surprising that in this era of the instantaneous flow of massive amounts of information, such a deception could be maintained for years. However, the core event, the bull's eye, was thousands of miles away, and we outsiders were seated on the outer ring. As I noted earlier, information about remote places is the easiest to massage, whether it be the success of an invasion or the efficacy of socialized medicine.

Unlike the Secretary of Defense, the managers of mutual funds are regularly audited, because investors spend billions of dollars on management fees, sales loads, and other charges. However, managed funds do no better than unmanaged funds, as I mentioned earlier   Even more amusing is that an unmanaged fund beat ninety percent of the managed funds during the decade from 1988 to 1998. Moreover, a fund that did better than its peers one year almost invariably did not repeat this triumph the next year, suggesting that the superior performance was due to chance, not wisdom. Seldom does the victor in the Super Bowl or World Series one year show up there the next year.

This should not come as a surprise. It is just another example of what statisticians call "regression to the mean." There is a tendency for a random quantity to approach its average value in the long run. Batting averages illustrate this phenomenon. Every year at the beginning of the baseball season several batters may have averages well over .400, but as the season progresses the averages settle down, the .400's disappear, and most players tend to be near.250.

Since we are not trained to pay attention to audits, the thousands of managed mutual funds stay in business, exchanging over a billion shares a day. We can't imagine that their managers, well dressed, well spoken, with splendid offices, cannot anticipate the future any better than we.

DON'T EXPOSE OUR SHAMANS

In truth, we do not want our shamans exposed. I recall the reception that the book, *The Experts,* by C. E. Pettit, received when it appeared in 1974. Pettit compiled some 2000 quotations covering over three decades of French and then American involvement in Vietnam. These came from press accounts, official reports, broadcast media, and government press releases. A few of the quotes are prescient, such as this from Senator Wayne Morse, Republican from Oregon, in 1954: "What is it we are going to fight for and to defend? I am a Senator and I don't know. The Democratic Senators on the Armed Services and Foreign Relations Committees don't know."

Most are off the mark, such as Secretary of State John Foster Dulles's comment, made a month later, "What we are trying to do is create a situation in Southeast Asia where the Domino Theory will not apply." The image of a long line of dominos falling dominated the perceptual option and helped set United States policy for decades. Our leaders, evidently unaware that China and Vietnam had been enemies for a millennium, were surprised when the two countries indulged in another war after we left. So much for dominoes.

Not everyone was surprised. A friend of mine of Chinese ancestry was of draft age during the Vietnam War. His father warned him to stay out of the army, "If the Vietnamese capture you, they'll kill you. They hate the Chinese."

Most of the quotations predict inevitable victory, if not soon, then before long — mentioning a "light at the end of the tunnel." Anyone reading them will wonder how so many people could be so wrong for so long.

The *New York Times* reviewed the book favorably:

> *Pettit has carefully refrained from writing much of anything beyond the brief foreword ... There is always the chance that the experts will produce yet another onset of that old fever. At the first sign we can reach into this volume and pop a few of their old words and prescriptions into the mouth, like anti-toxin pills.*

Publishers' Weekly was even more enthusiastic:

> *His cut-and-paste job (sans interpretations) gets his message across: there are no experts.*

But the review in *Best Sellers* was quite critical:

> *This is not a book but a mere collection of remarks made by various people who are dubbed 'experts' repeated with a sardonic sneer. The remarks are very brief, not well rounded or qualified — indeed hardly ever fair.*

Here we see the reviewers use the freedom we all have to interpret a thing however we wish to. We select the perceptual option most compatible with our model. I feel that the first review is accurate. The third reveals what I believe is a popular suspicion that an audit is mean-spirited. In any case, there was little interest in *The Experts* and it soon faded into oblivion. Laypersons may have thought, "So what else is new, we all make mistakes." Browse through it and decide for yourself; you may grow more wary of experts or more tolerant of their shortcomings.

Later C. Cerf and V. Navasky brought out *The Experts Speak,* revised in 1998, with a much broader scope than Pettit's *The Experts,* though it includes a long section on the Vietnam War. It quoted experts being wrong in fields as diverse as economics, politics, music, art, technology, war, and science. They mention an "Institute of Expertology." To become a member, you must submit an example of an expert being wrong. They distinguish three types of experts: Those who pronounce on the past, the present, or the future. It's hard to tell whether they are being facetious or are offering the first tentative steps toward a theory of expertise.

When I browse through its pages I get the impression that everyone is wrong all the time. But in the back of my mind is the hope that it is getting harder to find erroneous pronouncements: Don't we all learn from experience? Perhaps some patient social scientist will make an objective study of past utterances to see what fraction of the time experts are right, and if they are growing wiser, at least in some fields. It may even be possible to write a book titled *The Experts are Sometimes Right,* containing only correct predictions. In contrast to the pessimistic books on expertise, it could become a best seller.

Our reluctance to treat audits seriously may be sensible. That way we can live our lives in peace and pretend that the world is well managed by somebody else. That approach works most of the time. It doesn't work all the time, as New Orleans, the Iraq occupation, and the latest recession bear witness.

24 Spinoff and Side Effect

The four parts of impact; Spinoff; Side effect.

As we devise a plan we focus our minds on the goal, on the intended impact of our action. But as the action unfolds in the world, it generates an unanticipated impact of its own. Our creation drifts out of our control like a helium balloon whose string has slipped from our hand.

No wonder we meet an article headlined "Downside of Doing Good: Disaster Relief Can Harm" and learn that foreign aid can "sustain a war economy, legitimize outlaw authorities, and create mass refugee movements."

That we have traditionally ignored this part of impact is reflected in the lack of an English word meaning "unforeseen negative impact." For that matter, neither is there a word for "foreseen impact," the distinction between the two having until recently been unnecessary. But once again the large scale of our enterprises forces us to distinguish between them in order to give the unforeseen a place in the design of our grand projects.

THE FOUR PARTS OF IMPACT

The word "plan" describes the foreseen impact. In deference to the economists' "cost-benefit analysis," "cost" applies to the negative part, and "benefit" to the positive part. However, the terminology for the unforeseen impact is not as clearly developed.

For lack of a specific term for unforeseen impact, the word "surprise" will do. Plan and surprise together form the total impact.

SPINOFF

Just as the plan splits into positive and negative, so does the surprise. For the positive surprise I suggest the word "spinoff." The meaning of "spinoff" has been evolving as the need for a word denoting "positive unforeseen impact" grew.

"Spinoff" was not even listed in the dictionaries of 1950. By 1961 it did appear, but with a narrow technical meaning, "the transfer of a business owned by a corporation to a corporation it controls." By 1968, the meaning had broadened to describe "a new application or incidental result, especially if beneficial." So "spinoff" could include harmful impact.

A few years later "spinoff" took on a definitely positive tone. In 1976, NASA's annual report on the transfer of innovations in space technology to industrial, medical, and social applications was titled for the first time "*Spinoff.*" Earlier it had been called the *Technology Utilization Program Report*, hardly a catchy phrase. This shift justifies limiting the word to positive unforeseen impact; NASA wasn't going to advertise any negative unforeseen impact of its program. It understood how to use distortion by omission and commission. Now "spinoff" also refers to a TV show that grows out of another show.

SIDE EFFECT

The negative part of surprise is its "side effect." The recent history of this term also reveals our growing awareness of unforeseen impact. Like "spinoff," it did not appear in the dictionaries of 1950, but by 1961 it is to be found there, defined as "an effect of a drug other than the one it was intended to evoke." That side effect could be beneficial or injurious. By 1969 the negative connotation won out, with "side effect" defined as "a secondary, often injurious effect." So "side effect" refers only to the negative unforeseen impact.

All told, there are four types of impact from an action, with the foreseen (the plan) split into benefit and cost, and the unforeseen (the surprise) into spinoff and side effect.

Perhaps connected to the dramatic changes in the meanings of "spinoff" and "side effect" was the decline and fall around 1965 of the phrases "Yankee know-how" and "American ingenuity." The disappearance of a word or phrase is not recorded as conspicuously as the arrival of a new one. However, it would be easy with the aide of computers to spot the gradual decline of a word.

The histories of "spinoff" and "side effect" reflect our growing concern with unforeseen impact, as does the introduction of Environmental Impact Reports. When an idea, such as "unforeseen injurious consequences," becomes important, society provides a word for it. We are like those carpenters who, finding the word "beam" imprecise, use the words "stud," "joist," and "rafter" for vertical, horizontal, and sloping beams. The lack of a word may blur our thought, but if we need one we will devise it soon enough.

Even the unforeseen impact of our enterprises is large. The true cost of an action, composed of both traditional cost and side effect, can easily surpass the benefit, formed of traditional benefit and spinoff. In the enthusiasm of action, we focus on benefit, expect spinoff, minimize projected cost, and hope that side effect will take care of itself and, if not, that someone else downwind or downtime will deal with it.

25   The Scientific Method

Does smoking kill? Psychics and crime;
My encounter with ESP; Does remote prayer heal?
I study drunk and sober drivers; The dowsers.

So far I've mentioned the scientific method of settling issues only to serve as a contrast with the way we reason in life. In science and math there are clear-cut rules. In life anything goes. It is like playing a game in which the only restriction is that you cannot hit your opponent. You can lie, conceal, drown out, mislead, confuse, and no one will accuse you of committing a crime or not playing fair.

But the scientific method can settle issues that have traditionally been abandoned to rhetoric, in which the voice quality, choice of words, dress and charisma of the speaker may play a determining role. For instance, all but the last two of these questions can be addressed by science:

· Does smoking kill?

· Do psychics help solve crimes?

· Is there extrasensory perception (ESP)?

· Does remote prayer help patients?

· How dangerous is a drunk driver?

· Does dowsing for water work?

· Should the United States have intervened in Vietnam?

· Is there a God?

DOES SMOKING KILL?

This is our first question. The traditional argument used to go like this:

> *"Smoking isn't dangerous. Churchill always had a cigar in his mouth and he lived to the ripe old age of 93. Better than that, my Uncle Harry smoked three packs a day and lived to 102."*

Then came the rebuttal:

> *"U.S. Grant was a heavy cigar smoker and died of throat cancer at 63. Babe Ruth chewed tobacco and suffered the same fate at 53."*

So far it's a tie, two to two. Whoever had the wit to say something more won the match. That could be called "Truth through anecdote," which makes about much sense as settling an argument by a duel or a game of tennis.

In the scientific approach researchers followed the lives of thousands of smokers and nonsmokers, chosen as a fair sample from the general population. They then analyzed the data using statistics. This took time, money, and careful planning. The answer was that smoking does kill.

It may seem odd that what we see close up with our own eyes may not be the most reliable basis for our beliefs, for building our model of the world.

PSYCHICS AND CRIME

Our second question is, "Do psychics help solve crimes?"

As with the first question, this also can be treated by anecdotes. One side may mention a case where a psychic provided a key to solving a crime; the other, an instance where the psychic's visions wasted police efforts.

This question was answered in 1979 with the aid of the scientific method. Psychologists associated with the Los Angeles Police Department designed a clever experiment. Physical evidence from four crimes was placed in sealed envelopes. Twelve psychics offered information, first in response to the envelopes and then when their contents were revealed. The conclusion was,

> *The data does not support the contention that psychics can provide information leading to the solution of crimes. Many believed these cases might have been connected with the "Hillside Strangler." None were.*

Then in 1982 the same group conducted another experiment, comparing psychics with college students and homicide detectives. This time they found that,

> *The psychics generated lengthy discourses averaging a page and a half with dramatic and confident-sounding statements. The detectives produced on the average a quarter of a page of very terse statements. So did the students.*

> *Despite producing ten times as much information as the two comparison groups, the psychics were unable to produce information significantly better than the comparison groups.*

In 1994, a similar experiment in Great Britain, comparing three professional psychics with three students, concluded that,

> *Although the psychics made many more comments than the students, they were no more accurate. In short, the results provided no evidence to support the claims of the three psychics.*

Even so, one of the psychics soon after the experiment appeared on BBC, declaring that,

> *I have proved my psychic abilities. I did a test at the Department of Psychology at Hatfield University. They are thinking, "How does he do this?" I don't know how I do it but it does happen.*

One experiment was not enough. Further experiments were made to avoid small flaws in the design of earlier ones and to accumulate more evidence. Truth is an elusive prey.

You may think because I cite these experiments that I am opposed to psychics. I am not. I would be delighted if human beings had psychic powers. If so, I would certainly try to discover and develop my own. This takes us to the third question.

MY ENCOUNTER WITH ESP

"Is there extrasensory perception?" Do some people have the ability to send or receive information without the aid of physical means such as sound or radio waves?

This is a question in which I became personally involved. Charles Tart, a parapsychologist on my campus, devised a simple and elegant experiment to answer the question. He placed a person, called the "subject," in one room, where a random-number generator repeatedly produced one of the ten digits 0 through 9. The subject tried to transmit the digit to a person in another room, which was sealed off from any possible signal, either electro-magnetic or acoustic. Tart reported that the number of hits was significantly above the ten percent figure that mere guessing would be expected to yield.

When he studied the computer printout, he suspected that there might have been precognition as well, that is, more often than by chance the receiver anticipated the next digit before it was presented.

When he showed me the raw data I noticed that the number generator had a defect. It tended to repeat a digit immediately more than ten percent of the time. As a chemist would say, the test tube was dirty and the experiment, even though it might not have been influenced by the flaw, had to be repeated.

A few years later, he repeated the experiment. This time there was no sign of telepathy. The number of hits was very close to what mere chance would yield. Tart explained this failure to find evidence of "psi-hitting,"

> We had significantly less talented percipients. Why was
> this the case? We can offer no definitive answer, but a

few speculations may be in order. Because the scores in the first experiment were so high, it would be absurd to argue that the new results mean that the results of the first experiment were a statistical fluke ... Several people with close contact with students on the campus over the past three or four years have told us of a dramatic change in their attitude. In the last year or two, students have become more serious, more competitive, and more achievement-oriented than they were at the time of the first experiment. Such "uptight" attitudes are less compatible with strong interest and motivation to explore or develop a "useless" talent such as ESP.

The situation was also different for the students who ran the experiments. Those in the first experiment could legitimately feel that they were embarking on a new adventure. Despite our best efforts to create the same enthusiasm in the second group, there is no way we could deny that we were asking them to simply repeat an experiment designed and executed by others ... This could have been responsible for the relatively poor performance.

Even so, the second experiment casts a shadow over the first one. Science depends on repeated experiments producing consistent results. At this point it appears that there is no scientific evidence for the existence of mental telepathy.

That is not to rule out the possibility of telepathy. After all, it would be just another case of action at a distance. When I let go of a glass, the earth pulls it to the floor. How does it do this? How can one object pull another without the aid of a rope? Or how can a transmitter far away send a signal that I can pick up on my receiver? How does my horseshoe magnet attract paper clips? We are surrounded by mind-boggling miracles but don't notice them. We are jaded.

Since the brain produces an electro-magnetic field, which can be picked up by instruments that have no contact with the skin, I can imagine that it could transmit a signal at a distance. That would be just one more miracle. Even so, I would be surprised —

happily surprised — if it does. Astonishing claims demand strong evidence, not just hits a little above chance. If the data are so fragile that they require a sophisticated statistical test to show that more than mere chance is involved, I would not be convinced. The results of an experiment would have to be so overwhelming that they would convince me just by a quick glance at the numbers. Even so, I would want others to obtain the same results independently. In the meantime, I will assume that telepathy does not exist.

DOES REMOTE PRAYER HEAL?

"Does prayer by strangers help patients get well?"

Even this question can be addressed in the scientific way. A 1988 paper, "*Positive Therapeutic Effects of Intercessory Prayer in a Coronary Care Unit Population,*" reported on an experiment involving almost 400 patients in a San Francisco hospital. They were broken into two groups of roughly the same size. One group was prayed for by "born-again" Christians outside the hospital. The other was not. Each intercessor was told a patient's first name, diagnosis, and general condition. They prayed daily. Neither the patients nor the staff and doctors knew who was in which group.

It turned out that 85% of the prayed-for group had a "good hospital course," but only 73% of the control group. Only four of the first group had congestive heart failure, compared to 10 in the control group. Only two contracted pneumonia, as opposed to 7 in the control group. On several dozen other variables the outcomes were about the same. The study concluded, "Based on these data there seemed to be an effect, and that effect was presumed to be beneficial."

There was no conjecture on how prayer might have achieved its effect. Was it the direct action of the prayer on the patient or did it involve a God, who then acted? I find it perplexing that prayer seemed to have no effect on variables such as "unstable angina" and the most important one, "mortality." Perhaps if you look at enough variables, the sheer laws of probability may show that some will behave favorably.

A much larger double-blind experiment, called *Study of the Therapeutic Effects of Intercessory Prayer*, was conducted from January, 1998 to November, 2000. The final report appeared in 2006, with the conclusion,

> *Intercessory prayer had no effect on the coronary artery bypass group, but certainty of receiving intercessory prayer was associated with a higher incidence of complications.*

Since this experiment was large and well designed, we may assume that remote intercessory prayer does not help patients.

I STUDY DRUNK AND SOBER DRIVERS

"How dangerous are drunk drivers?"

This is a question I explored in research published in the journal *Alcohol, Drugs, and Driving*. I decided to compare the risk of drunk versus sober drivers. Since the data on fatal accidents is much more reliable than those on injury- or property-damage accidents, I decided to use just fatal accidents. Moreover, I wanted to estimate this risk as it varies throughout the day.

Luckily, computer printouts of traffic flow made estimating the number of cars on the roads fairly easy. However, I had no direct way of estimating what fraction of the drivers were sober and what fraction were drunk. I had to do this indirectly, by several methods, since I couldn't order a thousand randomly chosen cars to stop so I could run breathalyzer tests. In one approach, I looked at the data for two-car fatal accidents involving at least one drunk driver. Comparing the number of these accidents in which both drivers were drunk with the number in which one was sober and one was drunk, and then applying some probability theory and algebra to the data, I could estimate the fraction of drivers who were drunk.

I summarized my computations in the conclusion that at any time of day a drunk driver is about one hundred times as likely as a sober driver to be involved in a fatal accident.

THE DOWSER

Even the dowser question has been investigated scientifically. In the experiments with the dowser there was no evidence that it helped find water. However, that may not be the end of the issue. When the California Department of Transportation (CalTrans) was having trouble finding a suitable place for a rest stop, it called on one of its engineers, who was also a dowser, to find water along Insterstate 5. He succeeded, and that is why we have a rest area between Redding and Red Bluff.

The last two questions don't lend themselves to the scientific approach.

"Should the United States have intervened in Vietnam?"

In this case, we can run no experiments. The event happened once and cannot be repeated. Some claim that our involvement prevented Communist expansion in Asia. Others insist that it was a dreadful mistake, that we butted into a civil war. Historians and politicians will be haggling over this perceptual option for decades, arguing about a hypothetical "what if" world in which we never entered Vietnam. There may be no final answer.

The question, "Is there a God," lies outside the domain of science. It is a matter of faith that one believes there is and, similarly, a matter of faith that one believes there is not. Whatever the answer may be, it is not that crucial: there are atheists who do good and believers who do evil.

The scientific way is not easy. Some truths may be as hard as diamonds and not be easily accessible to mere mortals. Even if no one is trying to distort the core fact by omission or commission, the follower of the scientific method must exercise great care in drawing conclusions. That is one reason scientific journals referee papers. It is so easy to slip up and overlook a flaw or a gap, which in hindsight should have been obvious. This is true not only of arcane research into the secrets of atoms, genes, and stars, but also of the more homely investigations of the human condition.

Some issues can be settled by the scientific method, some not. It is the second type, the ones that cannot be tested by experiments, that invite the various ruses of commission and omission. Instead of vast gathering of data, double-blind comparisons with controls, and anonymous referees, these issues will be settled by charisma, rhetoric, and manipulation.

With practice, we can try to remember that difference. We may ask ourselves whether an issue is subject to the scientific method and request that the method be employed. If we decide that it lies outside the domain of the scientific method, then we can remember the dead-fish principle and the role of shamans.

26 Prophecy: Modeling the Future

The crystal ball; Checking up on an ad.

Mathematicians make predictions, but we call them "guesses" and "conjectures." A "guess" is an assertion we think may be true, but we have no evidence to back it up. A "conjecture" is more serious, for we have data to suggest that it is true. These predictions become the guiding force for research. If a prediction is wrong, little harm is done.

Predictions in the real world play a different role. If they turn out to be wrong, lives may be lost and businesses fail. You would think that because of this, forecasting would long ago have been subjected to substantial scientific scrutiny. This is not the case, though in recent decades it has become the object of some research.

THE CRYSTAL BALL

We have been so busy making predictions that we have not stopped to ask such simple questions as, "How well do we predict?" "How do we evaluate a forecaster?" and, perhaps the deepest question, "Is there a limit to our ability to see into the future?" This is like asking, "How far can we see into a fog?"

Science has discovered some limits: we cannot move faster than light, nor can we cool anything below - 460 degrees Fahrenheit. In mathematics we have discovered many other limits. For instance, it is impossible to draw a twenty-degree angle, using just unmarked dividers and an unmarked straightedge. (It is easy to draw a thirty-degree angle that way.)

There is likewise a limit to our prophetic ability. Knowing what it is may make us more humble as we plan our great gambles.

There are signs that the art of prophecy is finally being turned into a scientific discipline. For instance, the *Journal of Forecasting*, founded in 1982, describes methods of forecasting, case studies, and an occasional look at earlier forecasts. Browsing through its pages, however, I have seen no dramatic improvement in the accuracy of predictions.

We may feel that we see into the future more clearly than bygone seers. They depended on omens, the cries of birds, tea leaves, palm reading, the cracks in burned bones, or the positions of the planets. We have computers plus the benefit of a longer past to search for clues of what the future holds.

But are we wiser than the countless generations that have come and gone? Imagine ourselves back in the year 1900, when we were already quite modern. How much of the 20th century would we have foreseen? The two world wars? The Holocaust? The end of colonialism in Africa? Television? Antibiotics? The computer? The atom bomb? Do we think that, because we are more sophisticated, the 21st century holds fewer surprises? On January 1, 2000, how much of even the next few years could we have predicted? The spread of international terrorism? The invasion of Iraq? A massive worldwide recession?

Wars are the great earthquakes that reshape minds and nations. Yet, when we look back, we see that they are far from inevitable, hence not predictable. Different decisions by just a few leaders could have avoided the two world wars and certainly the Vietnam and Iraq wars. Historians may sketch realistic scenarios that "could have been" if those in power had chosen a slightly different path.

It doesn't require the efforts of many people to take a nation from peace to war. Hermann Goering, for one, saw how it was done by the Nazi hierarchy in 1939. In *Nuremberg Diary*, Gustav Gilbert, an American intelligence agent and psychologist, who had access to the Nazi bigwigs during the Nuremberg trial, recorded the technique, as Goering described it:

> *"I do not think that the common people are very thankful for leaders who bring them war and destruction. Why, of course, the people don't want war," Goering shrugged. "Why would some poor slob on a farm want to risk his life in a war when the best that he can get out of it is to come back to his farm in one piece. Naturally, the common people don't want war; neither in Russia nor in England nor in America, nor for that matter in Germany. That is understood.   But, after all, it is the leaders of the country who determine the policy and it is always a simple matter to drag the people along, whether it is a democracy or a fascist dictatorship ...."*

> *"There is one difference," I pointed out, "In a democracy the people have some say in the matter through their elected representatives, and in the United States only Congress can declare war."*

> *"Oh, that is well and good, but, voice or no voice, the people can always be brought to the bidding of the leader. That is easy. All you have to do is tell them they are being attacked and denounce the pacifists for lack of patriotism and exposing the country to danger. It works the same way in any country."*

The Iraq war of 2003 confirms Goering's formula.

How sophisticated are we?   The doors in our kitchen cupboards, being furnished with European hinges, spring shut, but we haven't the faintest idea how they work. We use zippers daily but can't make a sketch of how their parts mesh. It would take a long time to figure out how to make a combination lock. Though we are surrounded by countless devices, most far more sophisticated than those three inventions, our ways of thinking remain pretty much as they were centuries ago. We have become a knob-turning, button-pushing, dial-turning species with the accompanying illusion of being wiser than our ancestors.

As we bring forecasting into the realm of science, we quickly encounter an obstacle. Forecasting has a built-in handicap, a natural pressure to be wrong: we ask for a forecast only when we face the fuzzy part of the future, which inspires substantial uncertainty. We do not ask whether it will be hot in the Arizona desert in the middle of summer or whether the flag will have fifty stars two years from now. Instead we ask, "Will the interest rate be higher or lower in a year?" or "Will there be a job for me when I graduate?" We do not solicit a forecast when the future is likely to repeat the past. We want a forecast just when there is a good chance of its being wrong.

On the other hand, a forecaster has an advantage, for a prediction usually cannot be shown to be wrong at the time it is made. The world it is supposed to predict isn't here yet: it is a figment of the imagination. By the time it arrives, the forecast is forgotten. Contrast this with a perceptual option that models the present; it often can be checked quickly, for it concerns a world already here.

Forecasters may succumb to the temptation to view the future as being just like the past, only more so. This temptation is particularly strong when predicting an annual event described by a number, when one can look back at the numbers for past years. The mathematically inclined may even search for a formula that fits the trajectory and use it to extrapolate into the future.

For instance, picture yourself back in the year 1990 predicting future revenue of IBM. You would look at the following graph of annual revenues for the previous thirty years.

You could draw a smooth curve that passes close to all the points and extend it to the right more steeply. Or you could fit a simple mathematical formula that closely approximates the data. With either method, you would predict much higher revenues. IBM did make such a prediction, and it was wrong. Revenue shrank in 1991 and didn't return to the level of 1990 for five years. What went wrong? The introduction of the personal computer in the late '80s and early '90s had changed the traditional relation between IBM and its clients. IBM was taken by surprise. The future is not

simply an extension of the past, even when the past is described
by a pretty formula.

Even if we believe that it is hard to anticipate the future, we
still have enough confidence in our prophetic talent to fall into
a common trap.

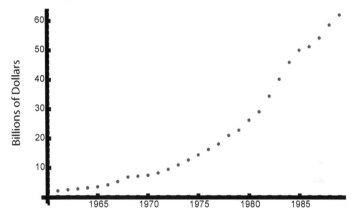

IBM Revenues 1960-1989: Data, IBM Archive; Mathmatica ™ Graph

When we hear the phrase, "This is a conservative prediction,"
what goes through our minds? Probably the feeling that things
cannot possibly be worse than what that prediction says. We act as
though the future is trapped somewhere between the most conservative and the wildest predictions, like peanut butter between two
slices of bread. What a smug view of our limited power as seers.

I learned the hard way to be leery of so-called "conservative"
investments. Years ago I bought a few shares of General Motors
and Pacific Gas and Electric, which a broker described as "conservative." PGE went through bankruptcy and General Motors,
outflanked by Toyota, made stupid decisions that threaten its
very survival

There is no such thing as a conservative prediction in matters
financial or political. There are only guesses made by people who
assume that no one will check whether the future turned out as
promised.

CHECKING UP ON AN AD

A forecast that involves simply predicting a number, such as the gross national product, automobile sales, or the price of a stock, invites mathematical finagling, or at least the appearance of objectivity and reliability that mathematics lends to a prediction. So, when I read in a full-page announcement by a brokerage firm in the August 19, 2001, *New York Times* that,

> *We believe the value of Standard and Poor's 500 stocks at the end of 2002 will be 50% above its index's level today*

I was impressed. Out of curiosity I saved the ad, with its prediction written in letters so large that it filled half the page. I didn't notice that at the bottom of the ad in small letters was a warning,

> *Actual developments are subject to risks, uncertainties, and other important factors.*

When the ad was published the index stood at 1182. The ad predicted a value of 1835, a bit more than a 50% increase. That the prediction was not "Somewhere around 1800 or 1900" but involved four-digit precision of 1835 and conveyed the impression it was the result of an analysis too deep to describe for the typical reader.

It turned out that on December 31, 2002, the index was at 880, more than a 25% decline from 1182. The "chief global strategist" had neglected to take into account a worldwide recession, and he could not have anticipated the destruction of the World Trade Center less than a month after he made his prediction. But could he have factored in the uncertainties arising from political instability and potential terrorism?

Is the prophet penalized for being wrong? No. He is not expected to anticipate the unanticipated. Are the recession and the September 11 disaster adequate explanation for the error in his prediction? How do we decide? How many of the million *Times* readers saved this prediction and checked up on its accuracy? Maybe the strategist pulled a number out of the air, not to make a serious prediction but to encourage investors to gamble in the stock market and generate commissions. In that case it should be judged as a lure, not as a prediction. We see here another obstacle to turning the art of prophecy into a science: It isn't clear whether a statement about the future is a genuine prediction or part of a sales pitch.

If we can't predict the music or the novels or the political movements of the future how can we expect to predict what will happen when so much of the future is shaped by the originality of over six billion people?

Even though predictions are unreliable, they have to be made. For instance, insurance companies or the Social Security Administration need predictions about the expected length of life, a forecast stretching almost a century into the future.

Does the future lie imbedded in the present, like seeds buried in the earth? Even if they are, we may not know which ones will be watered and, if watered, sprout, blossom, and produce fruit. If the future is not determined by the past and present, on what basis dare we forecast what it will be? It is one thing to predict the orbits of the planets, for they obey strict mathematical equations. It is quite another to predict the behavior of individuals and societies. There are no equations for that task.

Yet, when I saw the price of a barrel of oil rising in a smooth curve, I was sure that it would continue to get more expensive. When it was selling at $140 I bet my son that in six months it would still be above $100, while he said it would be nearer $60. I figured that rising world demand would continue to push the price upward. He felt that the high price was due to excessive speculation. He won the bet, for in six months a barrel was going for $67. How could I have been so wrong? Because out of nowhere came a world financial meltdown, which reduced the demand for energy. The future is made of surprises, as surely as an apple pie is made of apples.

As the financier George Soros put it,

> In human affairs, as distinguished from natural science ... our understanding is imperfect. [That] introduces an element of uncertainty that's not there in natural phenomena. So you can't predict human affairs in the same way you can natural phenomena.

We should stop acting as though we can.

27 Casual Audits

Camouflaged predictions; Watch the numbers;
An anniversary audit.

It's easy to find erroneous predictions. I'll look at a few in this
chapter, with their audits. In the next I will look at some more
formal audits. Here I take the anecdotal approach.

The cases I offer may convey the impression that all forecasts
are wrong. Of course, there are correct predictions. I already
mentioned Clubb's Vietnam prediction in Chapter 22. I. F. Stone
was right from the beginning of that war. Ivan Bloch, over a
decade before World War I, predicted, on the basis of an analysis
of the weapons available, in the next war the offense would be at
the mercy of the defenders' machine guns, the spade would play
as big a role as the gun, and war would reduce to a stalemate.

The worldwide financial panic of 2008 was far from a complete surprise. As far back as 1994 the General Accounting Office
had warned,

> *The sudden failure of a large U. S. dealer could cause*
> *liquidity problems in the markets and could pose risks*
> *to others . . . Intervention could result in a bailout paid*
> *for or guaranteed by the taxpayers.*

The government did not intervene, in part, because Alan Greenspan, head of the Federal Reserve, was reassuring,

> *Risks... are being regulated by private parties. There is nothing in Federal regulation which makes it superior to market regulation. Risk is part of life.*

As Senator Harbin observed about that testimony,

> *He had a way of speaking that made you think he knew exactly what he was talking about at all times. He was the Oracle, and who were you to question him?*

Here we see the shaman in action.

But the awareness of an impending disaster was not limited to the Accounting Office. One day I was chatting with a teller, who said, "For six years I worked for a mortgage lender. I knew from day one that it would end in calamity."

Barack Obama, months before the Iraq war, warned,

> *Even a successful war against Iraq will require an occupation of undetermined length, at undetermined cost, with undetermined consequences. It will only fan the flames of the Middle East, encourage the worst, rather than the best, impulses of the Arab world, and strengthen the recruitment arm of Al Qaeda. I'm opposed to dumb wars.*

To cite just one more accurate prediction, I mention David Sarnoff's view in 1916 of the future of broadcasting, when radio was still in its "headphone infancy":

> *I have in mind a plan of development, which would make radio a "household utility" in the same sense as the piano or phonograph. The idea is to bring music into the home by wireless. The same principle can be extended to lectures at home, events of national significance, baseball scores. Farmers could enjoy concerts and lectures.*

Implementing his vision, he founded RCA.

It would be useful to find out why some prognosticators are repeatedly right well above chance. Up to now research has focused instead on the forces that drive people to make erroneous forecasts.

That said, I will take a look at the more common case, where predictions made by experts, either professionals or shamans, turn out to be far off the mark.

In a "Pundit Scorecard" Brill's magazine reported on the accuracy of the five talking heads who weekly yell at each other on TV's McLaughlin Group. They were right on 80 predictions, wrong on 85, for a batting average of about 48%. That means all five pundits could have been replaced by a single penny. Tossing a penny 165 times, however, would not provide as entertaining a program.

As I mentioned in Chapter 14, meteorologists take their predictions seriously, prefixing them with their likelihood of being correct. Oddly, when predicting what may happen outside of the weather, a meteorologist reverts to the primitive "all or nothing" form, claiming "it will happen" or "it will not happen."

The preface to *Global Weather Prediction*, a book published in 1970 about the proceedings of a 1966 conference, includes this forecast:

> *Within the next decade there will be a revolution in the science of weather prediction, for within five to ten years it should be possible to make accurate ten-to-fourteen day weather forecasts. This amounts to a quantum jump beyond current forecasting ability.*

In spite of the use of weather satellites, this jump has yet to occur. Some meteorologists believe that we may never be able to predict further ahead than we can now, since small changes in temperature, humidity, or sunspots can cause large-scale changes in the weather days later. Similar obstacles may limit predictions in human affairs.

CAMOUFLAGED PREDICTIONS

Most predictions are smuggled into discussions of controversial issues. They are not prefaced by "I hereby predict that ..." or "Though I have been wrong fifty per cent of the time ..." or "There is a forty percent chance that ..." When a person who we think is wiser than we announces a vision of things to come, we are overcome by the magic of well chosen words, by the assurance of a calm, confident voice, by the majesty of office, and by our desire to peer into the mysterious realm of the future. Under such a spell it is hard to distinguish prediction from sales pitch from fact. That an utterance is a prediction, not a statement about the present, can easily slip by us. It is this blurring of present and future that permits a newspaper to run a front page story beginning with the headline, "Head of Federal Reserve Predicts Recession," as though the prediction assures us that a recession is coming.

The *New York Times* index is not divided into two sections, an Index of Actual Events and an Index of Predicted Events. Since the heading "predictions" is not even in the index, it is difficult to review past predictions and see how they turned out.

The history of a major controversy provides enough examples to show that statements about the future may be even more common than those about the present. The debate about whether to build the supersonic transport, SST, which began in 1967 and ended in 1971, is typical. Since the predictions made then can be checked now, it is worth examining this case. A few quotes I found in files of the *New York Times* are typical.

> · Sir John Elliot: "Just as the present fleet of jets threw the old piston-powered planes into the second line, so will the SST relegate the current jets to secondary ones. Travel will be cheaper than we ever dreamed."

> · R. J. Benecchi, President of Aerospace Group of Aeronca: "The SST is a necessity — if not today, certainly ten years hence when the mass of international traffic will require faster vehicles and new traffic lanes. The SST will fly irrespective of what we do."

> · President Richard Nixon, after the United States Senate decided to discontinue research on SST: "What is involved here is not just 150,000 jobs which will be lost if we don't build it, not just the fact that billions of dollars in foreign exchange will be lost."

> · Karl G. Harr, Jr., President of the Aerospace Industries Associates: "We stand in danger of doing irreparable harm to the aerospace industry."

Even so, the United States did not build the SST. France and England jointly developed SST, but the few Concordes built flew at a loss and no airline voluntarily bought any. In spite of the gloomy predictions, the United States did not lose its leadership in aviation, and Boeing for years had a backlog of unfilled orders. Finally, in 2003, the Concordes were taken out of service and lodged in museums.

Not only specialists, with presumed expertise, predict. The average person also has visions of things to come, as a glance through a compilation of Gallup or Harris polls shows. In October, 2003, a Harris poll asked, "How likely do you think it is that the United States will get bogged down for a long time in Iraq and not be able to create a stable government there?" The response was: Very Likely, 42%; Somewhat likely, 32%; Not very likely, 14%; Not at all likely, 7%; Not sure, or refused, 5%. Incidentally, 95% of the respondents had an opinion, showing how rich are our models of the future. Moreover, what makes some respondents say "very likely" and others "not at all likely?" Does the answer say more about Iraq or about the personality of the person polled, being a pessimist or optimist by nature?

There is a general tacit agreement not to look back on such polls or any predictions, but not just to avoid embarrassment. By not examining the past, we can pretend we and our leaders are reliable seers. The leaders, in turn, are free to prophesy with the assurance that their errors will not be held against them.

We laypersons in the outer rings, watching the world turn, might expect about half of the predictions to be wrong. The reason for this is simple. Predictions are usually made in the midst of a controversy. There are usually two sides, and we would expect that each side makes the same number of predictions. If the predictions on one side tend to be right and those on the other side to be wrong, that would give us a rule-of-thumb guess that about fifty percent would be right. Perhaps someone of a curious bent may refine and test this conjecture by rummaging through the Congressional Record, old newspapers, and magazines.

WATCH THE NUMBERS

To strip away some of the magic from predictions "based on a computer" I will recall an article I wrote, called *Opinion In, Opinion Out,* which appeared in *Technological Forecasting and Social Change* in 1981. First, though, I call attention to the difference between a program for a computation and the numbers that are fed into that program.

Whoever is using a computer first writes a program that tells the computer what to do when it is given some numbers. Then the operator feeds the computer some numbers on which the computer grinds away with incredible speed and accuracy. Anyone who has used software to fill out the 1040 tax form has been such an operator. The software is the program. Each taxpayer inserts the numbers. Bill Gates and a bus driver insert quite different numbers.

In 1973 M. Bunge published *A Decision Theoretic Model of the American War in Vietnam,* in which he deduced that "negotiation" would have been a better strategy for achieving our goals.

His model listed six goals, such as "checking communist expansion" and "saving American prestige," with corresponding side effects, namely the opposites of the goals. There were two means, "negotiating" and "total war." He assigned each goal a number describing its "utility" or "importance," together with the probability of its being achieved by each means. Then, as in Chapter 14, he computed the expected value of the two means and concluded that negotiation was the preferable strategy, as surely as 0.51 is larger than -0.30.

Keeping the same means and the same goals, I used his program. However, there is a great leeway in assigning the numbers that describe the "utilities" of the goals and the probabilities that a given means will achieve each goal. I showed that a reasonable case could have been made during the war, using numbers as plausible as Bunge's, that demonstrated total war is the preferable strategy, as surely as 0.80 is larger than -0.763.

The objective part of the model, its program, its structure, consisted of the two means and six goals. But the subjective part, the perceptual option, enters when we choose the numbers to measure utilities and probabilities. Bunge's model was so simple it did not need a computer. That exposed the role of the operator's opinions. When the model is so complicated that a computer is required, then the role of the operator is hidden.

I observed in my article, "Just as two rational lawyers can support opposing clients, so can two rational decision theorists." That assertion applies also to two forecasters.

AN ANNIVERSARY AUDIT

Sometimes a significant anniversary occasions an informal audit. This was the case with the North American Free Trade Agreement (NAFTA), which went into force January 1, 1994. Its tenth anniversary was marked by attempts to decide whether it was, on the whole, a success or a failure. The verdicts were as diverse as the predictions made a decade earlier.

A sample of the speeches recorded in the *Congressional Record — Senate* for September 24, 1993 shows the variety of expectations.

Senator Riegle was opposed to the treaty:

> *That is precisely the problem we face with NAFTA — the threat of draining jobs out of the United States ... At its heart it is much more an investment agreement than it is a trade agreement, because NAFTA provides important new protections for United States investments in Mexico ... What kind of guarantees do workers get? What kind of guarantees are provided for the environment?*

On the other hand, we find Senator Durenberger optimistic:

> *I happen to be of the opinion that most jobs that will leave America have already left, or their companies would not be here at this stage of the game, and that the notion that NAFTA is going to be an additional job drain defies the reality of economics.*

Plugging "NAFTA" into Lexis-Nexis ten years later, I found retrospectives, some cheering the agreement, some condemning it, and some neutral. That was to be expected with an action that had so many different impacts. We were in the world of incomparables.

The economist Joseph Stiglitz, winner of a Nobel Prize, in an article titled "The Broken Promise of NAFTA," summarized the verdicts:

> *Today, most trade economists read the evidence as saying that NAFTA has worked: intra-area trade and foreign investment have expanded greatly. Trade skeptics and anti-globalists look at the same history and feel no less vindicated ... Look at the contraction of manufacturing employment in the United States. As for the environment, go ... where the maquiladores cluster, and take a deep breath.*

The perceptual option depends on what the viewer emphasizes. The total impact of NAFTA, which involves jobs, environment, and standard of living, cannot be measured by a single number, though these factors, taken individually, may be. Besides, during the ten years of NAFTA, many jobs in the United States and even in Mexico emigrated to China, a complication not foreseen in 1993, but muddying the audit. The audit of such a program cannot be as simple as determining whether a business had a profit or a loss. There is no single bottom line.

KEEP IT SIMPLE

The calculations in our Vietnam example did not need the service of a computer. However, more sophisticated models do not seem to give more accurate predictions even though they require the assistance of a computer.

In an article titled "Accuracy in Forecasting," which appeared in the *Journal of Forecasting* in 1984, E. Mahmoud concluded that, "Simple forecasting methods perform more accurately than, or at least as accurately as, sophisticated methods."

In spite of all the sophisticated techniques developed in the following years, S. Makridakis observed in the same journal in 2000,

> *Statistically sophisticated or complex methods do not necessarily provide more accurate forecasts. The strong empirical evidence, however, has been ignored by theoretical statisticians who have been hostile to empiri-*

cal verifications. Instead they have concentrated their efforts in building more sophisticated models without regard to the ability of such models to more accurately predict real-life data.

The phrase "empirical verification" means "checking up on past predictions by an audit," a thankless task unlikely to earn professional advancement or the Nobel Prize in economics. That such audits offer little reward is implied in this observation of Michel Godet in the *Journal of Forecasting*:

The economic history of industrial society has been marked by repeated forecasting errors. What is serious is not so much the existence of errors as the systematic ignoring of past errors when new forecasts are made.

In other words, the learning curve seems to be a horizontal line.

In *The Death of Economics*, the economist P. Ormerod observed,

The models may seem impressive and intimidating when their mathematical specifications are set down on paper, but when it comes to their use in forecasting, they are so unreliable that virtually no operator dares allow the model loose on its own.

More generally, he warned,

The temptation to use mathematics is irresistible for economists. It appears to convey the appropriate air of scientific authority and precision to economists' musings. More subtly, it hides the implications of many assumptions, which are made routinely in professional work.

Dare we conclude that using mathematics to explain or predict social phenomena is a sign that a shaman may be operating?

An academic specialist in urban planning, M. Wachs, in an article entitled "Forecasts in Urban Transportation Planning: Uses, Methods, and Dilemmas," described the same phenomenon:

Maintaining an illusion of technical objectivity by placing computerized forecasts of travel demand and cost in a central position in policy debates, transit officials politely disguise the fact that allocations of billions of dollars in grants for new systems are politically motivated.

He goes on to make a much broader comment:

> *I am convinced that most of the forecasts used in the planning of America's rail transit systems are statements of advocacy rather than unbiased estimates produced by politically neutral applied social scientists. I believe that similar case studies could be produced from other sectors in which forecasting routinely plays an important role in policy debates: energy, environmental planning, and housing, for example.*

In a study of forecasting the demand for new consumer communication and information services, J. Carey and M. Elton questioned the value of experts' predictions:

> *There is no evidence that experts' guesses are better than anyone else's. Indeed, there is some reason to expect that they may be worse, because they are often biased by personal interest in the success of the technology or service.*

James Cayne, chief executive at Bear Stearns, while testifying at a trial to find out whether his firm is obligated to repay a client who lost millions on investments based on its forecasts, asserted that those forecasts should not be taken seriously: "... [Economists] don't really have a good record as far as predicting the future. I think it is entertainment."

These revelations should leave us laypersons bewildered. Must we admit to ourselves that the experts who we imagine know more than we and ponder more deeply than we are merely shamans or deceivers? If so, our future becomes just one big gamble, an all-embracing GRIMP. Our motto will then be reduced to "Let them do it and let's see what happens." But we are not so helpless. We can challenge the experts; we can examine their record and question their reasoning. Surely many of us can make the time to do this.

For now, we can at least be on guard when we hear a prediction, and remember that it is not a statement of fact. When we hear a sentence using the future tense, we should automatically discount it. Until forecasting is subject to methodical study we may want to collect some predictions on our own and check how they turn out. For instance, the Iraq war is a rich source. So is Afghanistan.

28 Serious Audits

You can't look back; You can't outsmart the future.

An essential feature of the Christmas holiday is the editorial bemoaning its materialism. This ritual has become part of the festivities along with the Yule stocking, the decorated tree, and Santa Claus. A week later comes New Year's Day with its customs, one of which is a look back at the fate of predictions made in the past year. That is as close as we come to a methodical evaluation of prophets and their prophecies. This audit usually focuses on economic seers and is relegated to the financial pages. Politicians are exempt from such a checkup.

YOU CAN LOOK BACK

There are, however, objective, scholarly studies of predictions, designed not to entertain, but to determine their accuracy. These reports are safely tucked away in such journals as *Social Problems, Econometrica*, and the *Journal of Personality and Social Psychology*, which we are not likely to find in an airport magazine rack. In spite of the diversity of their subjects, the conclusions are similar, as the following fair sample shows.

I will start with the oldest one I have come across, made in 1938, but as pertinent as any made today. Again it concerns the stock market, which is rich in verifiable predictions because they are expressed in numbers. In "Can Stock Market Forecasters Forecast," A. Cowles, III, analyzed the efforts of sixteen leading financial services, twenty-four financial publications, and twenty insurance companies to foretell which securities would rise or the general course of the stock market.

He showed that the results were a little worse than those that would have been achieved by random choices. He concluded,

> *Statistical tests of even the best individual records failed to demonstrate that they exhibited skill and indicated that they more probably were the results of chance. There is evidence that the least successful records are worse than what could reasonably be attributed to chance.*

That could just as well have been written in 2001, for *USA Today* on July 9, 2001, published an article with the headline, "Experts' stock picks lag market," reporting that "43 of 50 stocks recommended at the beginning of this year by 10 strategists polled are down, with an average 22% decline. That's worse than Standard and Poor's 500's 10% fall and the Dow's 5% dip. Eleven of the 50 stocks fell more than 50%." The strategists' alibi may be that 2001 was an unusual year, but it is usually the case that a year is unusual. Perhaps some scholar may wish to determine the odds that the next year will be unusual.

The study by Cowles was based on thousands of stock recommendations. Out of curiosity I looked at a few of the recommendations in a monthly newsletter a broker sent me. If I had followed its advice, I would have lost ten percent of my investment in a mere thirty days, even though the layout of the newsletter, being attractive and in several colors, had a convincing air.

In "An Example of Misplaced Confidence in Experts," Cocozza and Steadman in 1978 investigated the skill of psychiatrists in predicting the dangerousness of criminal defendants. Their predictions play a role in dealing with bail and parole.

Comparing the behavior of 96 defendants judged dangerous with that of 70 judged not dangerous, the authors found no statistically significant difference and decided that,

> *The profession of psychiatry is seen by society as possessing the special knowledge necessary to make these complex assessments. It is the psychiatrist who is identified in the mental health laws as the expert in the prediction of dangerousness. Our findings seriously question the existence of any such special knowledge. They clearly indicate that no such expertise exists and the attempt to apply this supposed knowledge to predict who will be dangerous results in complete failure. Psychiatrists may be acting more as seers than as scientists in predicting dangerousness.*

If this conclusion is confirmed by other studies, what is the court to do when setting bail or deciding about parole? Flip a coin? Though compatible with the principle that justice should be blind, it would mock the sober atmosphere of a courtroom. Even the defendant would object. So the custom of calling in the psychiatrist makes good sense. This happens to be one of those occasions when we must call upon the service of a shaman to help our tribe manage our affairs in a seemingly orderly manner.

I turn now to a study of experts in a quite different field, namely those individuals in think tanks, universities, or international agencies, who earn their bread by analyzing trends. Psychologist P. Tetlock, in 1998, in "Close-Call Counterfactuals and Belief-System Defenses: I Was Not Almost Wrong but I Was Almost Right," studied the predictions of diplomatic and military historians and political scientists about the Soviet Union, made in 1988, about South Africa, in 1990, and about Quebec, in 1992.

Though he was interested mainly in how experts behave when wrong, he noted that they were right only slightly more than half the time. Almost as many respondents as not thought that the Soviet Communist Party would remain in power in 1993, that neofascism would prevail in South Africa by 1994, and Quebec would secede by 1997.

Experts who assigned confidence estimates of at least 80% to their predictions were wrong more than 55% of the time. Many of them said they were basically correct, for the event "almost occurred." For instance, they would have been right if the hardliner coup in the Soviet Union had succeeded.

Tetlock remarked,

> *Indeed, expertise seemed most strongly associated with hubris. Experts predicting in their specialization differed from experts trespassing into alien domains primarily in the confidence they expressed in their prediction, not in their ability to foresee trends.*

In this trait, they are reminiscent of the psychics of Chapter 25.

The conclusion Tetlock drew may apply more generally than he intended:

> *It is arguably unfair to criticize our respondents for their lackluster predictive performance. World politics may pose an insurmountably indeterminate task in which one quickly reaches the point of diminishing marginal returns for increments in expertise. It may be impossible to perform better than chance in anticipating many political and economic events.*

And that raises yet another question; What does "better than chance" mean? That's another challenge for scholars.

YOU CAN'T OUTSMART THE FUTURE

Tetlock is not the first to suggest that we may be able to predict only so well. P. Ormerod, in *The Death of Economics*, in 1994, which I already cited, observed,

> *Economic forecasts are the subject of open derision. Throughout the Western world, their accuracy is appalling. Within the past twelve months alone forecasters have failed to predict the Japanese recession, the strength of the American recovery, and the depth of the collapse of the German Economy.*

Writing in *Principles of Forecasting*, D. Ahlburg made a similar observation in another area:

The experience of using experts in population forecasting is similar to that in other fields of forecasting where expert opinion has been shown to add little to forecast accuracy.

It is so easy to find such pessimistic admissions, that it is tempting to reach a pessimistic generalization. For the record, here is another one, on international relations, supporting the generalization. In "The Future of World Politics," which appeared in the journal *International Security*, Robert Jervis explained

...why prediction is so difficult in world politics. Among the reasons: multiple factors are usually at work, actors learn, small events can affect the course of history and, most importantly in this context, many well-established generalizations about world politics may no longer hold.

This sounds like the reason predictions about the weather have a limited range.

I could extend this list and publish another book like Pettit's, even with the same title, *The Experts*, but the point is already clear. I invite anyone to browse through the references in such places as the *Journal of Forecasting*. It seems that the field of prophecy in human affairs is the natural habitat of shamans. The few cases I have cited could be the beginning of a fascinating research project.

Given that forecasts by individuals are unreliable, forecasters introduced a refinement, called Delphi, involving a "consensus of experts." However, as reported in *Forecasting in the Social and Natural Sciences,* in 1987,

It doesn't work especially well as a forecasting tool; there is nothing about the consensus judgments of experts that makes their forecasts any more reliable than those obtained by other, even less involved, means.

No wonder some professional forecasters who advise business and government have switched from predictions to offering scenarios. Instead of trying to predict what will happen, they more humbly provide management with a variety of scenarios of what could happen. This, like Rubin's quantifying the odds, helps planners remain flexible. At least it lifts their minds out of a rut and reminds them how sensitive the future is to the unforeseen, or more simply, how sensitive the future is to the future.

No wonder that the acronym WAG has entered the deliberations of those who must plan for the future. Standing for "Wild Ass Guess," it is a companion for PFA, which we already met in Chapter 10. WAG should be stamped on predictions of what will happen when we toss a trillion dollars at a recession or spend it on the occupation of an oil-rich country.

The future is a great equalizer: both expert and layperson stand bewildered before it, both turned into dilettantes. It is as if there is no bull's eye, and the layperson does not have the usual alibi, "surely the insider knows more than I do." There may be no insider. In that case, we will have to identify an expert by secondary characteristics, such as the ability to project conviction, a sign of the shaman, not of the professional.

CONCLUSIONS

29 The Action Syndrome

The action syndrome: benefits; The moment of decision; The syndrome sustains.

Now I come to the "great magnifier." I discovered it by looking within myself as I made decisions and acted, but I conjecture that it seizes professional, shaman, and layperson alike when they undertake an action. It well may be the strongest distorter of all those influences that shape our models and choices.

I write this as outsider to outsider, bypassing experts. You can test my observations against your own experience. Maybe psychologists have studied the phenomenon, maybe not. Once again, if I step into a field owned by some specialty, I apologize. We laypersons have a right to communicate directly with each other without seeking the blessings of an expert.

A psychologist told me to omit this chapter, calling it "pop psychology." Well, he doesn't own the rights to comment on that peculiar and mysterious organ, the human brain. Novelists, poets, and playwrights do that all the time.

Moreover, I have the right to look into my own brain, and watch the way I think. I'm an expert on that. And I have the right to watch close-up how others behave. I don't need to take Psych

101 before I collect evidence, however anecdotal, and devise a theory, however small its basis.

I give readers the chance to mull over this chapter for themselves, based on their own experience. This is consistent with my goal of shrinking the role of expertise and expanding the faith of us laypersons in our own intuition. This does not mean that I am proposing that we carry out a heart bypass, launch a rocket to Mars, or build a bridge across the Bering Strait.

THE ACTION SYNDROME: BENEFITS

I wrote about my conjecture in *Strength in Numbers*, to explain the depth of passion that infuses the "math wars," that century-old battle between "back to basics" and "teach understanding." I call it the "action syndrome." It enables us to act, whether to create or to destroy. It helps reduce countless options to one. It enables a person who must act, whom I call an "actor," to commit utterly to this one option, to suppress doubt. It alters the actor's inner models of present and future to sustain dedication. Whether the action is wise or foolish, the action syndrome permits the actor to focus in pursuit of a goal.

The action syndrome is analogous to what physicians call the "generalized adaptation syndrome," which is the body's response to stress. Because of this similarity, it is worth noting the basic features of the "stress syndrome."

The stress syndrome describes how the body protects itself when disturbed by some stress, such as injury or disease or fatigue. More blood becomes available to the muscles, white blood cells are supplied to fight infection, and an inflammatory barrier forms around an injury.

Complex and automatic, the syndrome has been essential to the survival of the species. It is divided into three stages: alarm, resistance, and exhaustion. For instance, in the first stage persons can lift a weight they could not lift before. But the syndrome is not perfect. The response may even be a disease, such as a destructive inflammation, which damages the body it is supposed to protect.

The action syndrome, on the other hand, is an automatic, unconscious response of the mind to a challenge, enabling the individual to act in spite of fear and uncertainty. It transforms perception and prediction and simplifies choice in such a way that the person with the need to act can act. The actor can "make up his mind," be "single-minded," not of "half a mind," nor of "two minds." Under its influence perceptions seem flawless, and predictions certain.

The action syndrome may be thought of as self-hypnosis, as necessary for action as is the stress syndrome for physical survival. Originally, it may have served only as a survival mechanism, when choice and decision concerned simple challenges. But even in these times, it is critical in any act of consequence, marking the transition from detachment to attachment, from the hesitant "I think I shall do it" to the firm "I shall do it."

The action syndrome focuses the mind, as the stress syndrome focuses the body. It permits action to begin through decision, supports the action over time, and renders the completed action successful in the eyes of the actor.

The action syndrome polarizes the mind as a magnetic field aligns iron filings. This polarization appears in the form of an initial conversion followed by a doubt-suppressing will to act, described by such words as stubborn or persevering, close-minded or dedicated, monomaniacal or tenacious.

The action syndrome is not triggered by a hypothetical choice, any more than the stress syndrome is by talk about a hypothetical injury. It requires confrontation with a choice and an action that carry risk. Nor should it be viewed as just a part of the adversary process, with its tendency to polarize opponents. It serves even the isolated actor: the hiker lost in a storm, the lone sailor circumnavigating the globe, the scientist trying to wrest a secret from the universe.

Before commitment, the actor remains free to weigh risk and gain, to imagine the obstacles to success, to entertain alternatives. But the thinker, in order to become the actor, must leave the state of broad reflection, fix upon a single course in spite of any misgivings, and pass into a state of dedication, certain in his choice. The action syndrome facilitates this transition from observer to actor, as real as the metamorphosis of a caterpillar into a butterfly.

The action syndrome compensates for the quirk that circumstance often tends to favor the failure rather than the success of an enterprise. For success many things must go well. Just as a machine may not function if one part breaks, the failure of even one gamble may doom an enterprise. To compensate for this vulnerability, the action syndrome supports optimism.

THE COSTS

The action syndrome can be seen as a disease that diminishes wisdom. In this it resembles the worst features of the stress syndrome. The very response to stress may be a disease, a patient-induced disease, the damage caused not by an injury but by overreaction to that injury.

Inflammation, the body's first defense against infection, can get out of control and lead to heart attacks, colon cancer, or damage to the brain. When we call upon cortisone to suppress an inflammation, we are really trying to turn off the stress response. Just as there are times when the body should turn off that response, there are times when the mind must suppress the action response, for instance, in order to replace an emotional reaction by a calm analysis of alternatives.

EXAMPLES

A conversation between Xerxes and his advisor, Artabanus, as reported by Herodotus, reveals the role of the syndrome in undertaking a commitment. Artabanus said,

> It is best for men, when they take counsel, to be timorous, and imagine all possible calamities, but when the time for action comes, then to deal boldly."

Xerxes replied,

> Fear not all things alike, nor count up every risk. For if in each matter that comes before us you look to all possible choices, you will never achieve anything. Success attends those who act boldly, not those who weigh everything and are slack to venture. Great empires can only be conquered by great risks.

That advice shows both the value and the risk inherent in the action syndrome, since under its sway Xerxes, instead of expanding his empire, weakened it.

The action syndrome works through a mixture of suppression, distortion, and focusing, which induces a simplified view of cause and effect. In particular it suppresses concern for possible impacts, especially side effect. As Xerxes warned, no one could act if obliged to anticipate every side effect.

The defense offered by an expert who favored an air strike during the Cuban missile crisis is typical. When asked by President Kennedy what the Soviet response might be, the expert replied

I think they'll knock out our missile bases in Turkey.

What then?

Under our NATO treaty we'd be obligated to knock out a base in the Soviet Union.

"What will we do then?"

Then we hope everyone will cool down and want to talk.

The President, who had little faith in experts, pursued other options. After the failure of the Bay of Pigs invasion of Cuba, he reflected,

How could I have been so far off base? All my life I've known better than to depend on experts. How could I have been so stupid, to let them go ahead?

THE MOMENT OF DECISION

At the moment of decision, the syndrome induces a sense of relief and confidence, while it blots out the discarded alternatives as though a storm had passed and is followed by an intense calm. Choice, perception, and prediction all fall into line to support commitment. But the syndrome aids action in subtler ways. It permits the actor to cross certain barriers without even noticing them, such as the choice between incomparables.

The transition from non-action to action depends on a leap of faith. The actor, who moves from one state to the other, must cross an unavoidable gap hidden in what is often referred to as "the moment of decision." Peel off the layers of decision, the perceptions of past, present, and future, the choices between incomparables, the winnowing of possibilities down to a single action, and at the center lies ... a mystery. Under the influence of the action syndrome, we are unaware of it just as we are unaware of the blind spot in our vision that corresponds to the place where the optic nerve enters the retina. This gap marks the end of deliberation and the beginning of commitment.

That final leap follows several smaller steps that could not bear close cross- examination: the choice between incomparables, the balancing of incalculable risks, the prediction of the unknowable. But it is the great leap of the final decision, where the gamble is finally taken, that requires and enables the actor to reach a new state of consciousness.

No matter how meticulously we record the decision process, even in ourselves, there will inevitably be a gap corresponding to the moment of the leap, which amounts to a blank in the narrative.

The leap may even take on a divine form, as it did for President McKinley, when he decided to take the Philippines after the Spanish-American War.

When next I realized that the Philippines had dropped into our laps I confess I did not know what to do with them. I sought counsel from all sides. I walked the floor of the White House night after night until midnight; and I am not ashamed to tell you, gentlemen, that I went down on my knees and prayed Almighty God for light and guidance. And one night late it came to me this way ... I don't know how it was, but it came ... that there was nothing left for us to do but to take them all.

In this case God helped bridge the gap.

Freud was more down to earth, assigning to the unconscious the role that McKinley gave to God.

When making a decision of minor importance, I have always found it advantageous to consider all the pros

and cons. In vital matters, however, such as the choice
of a mate or a profession, the decision should come from
the unconscious, from somewhere within ourselves. In
the important decisions of our personal life, we should
be governed by the deep inner needs of our nature.

Facing the gap more directly, President Kennedy admitted,

The essence of ultimate decision remains impenetrable
to the observer — often, indeed, to the decider himself.
There will always be the dark and tangled stretches in the
decision-making processes — mysterious even to those
who may be most intimately involved.

Whether labeled divine insight, the work of the unconscious,
or the dark stretch, the gap is crossed with the aid of the action
syndrome.

THE SYNDROME SUSTAINS

The syndrome not only allows action to begin but it sustains
the actor's faith during the action. The world model, the perceptual options, the predictions are all slanted to maximize the
energy available to the action. As light from the stars bends as it
passes near the sun, so the world is warped as it passes near a
person in the state of action.

While the conversation between Xerxes and his advisor shows
how a man of action approaches a decision, the following conversation between Napoleon and his adviser, Caulaincourt, shows
how he manages to persevere, even in adversity. This exchange
took place during the Russian campaign of 1812, as the French
lingered in Moscow.

"What do you call our difficulties?" Napoleon asked, with
an air of irritation. "The winter," I answered, "is a big
difficulty, to begin with; the lack of stores, of horses for
your artillery, of transport for your sick and wounded,
the poor clothing for your soldiers. Every man must have
a sheepskin, stout fur-lined gloves, a cap with ear-tabs,

warm boot-socks, heavy boots to keep his feet from getting frostbitten. You lack all this. Not a single calkin has been forged to rough-shoe the horses; how are they going to draw the guns? There is no end to what I could tell your Majesty on this subject. Then there are your communications; the weather is still fine, but what will it be in a month, in a fortnight, perhaps in even less?"

"So you think I am leaving Moscow?" he demanded.

"Yes, Sire."

"That is not certain. Nowhere shall I be better off than in Moscow. You do not know the French. They will get all they need; one thing will take the place of another. The extreme rigors of winter do not come on in twenty-four hours. Although we are less acclimatized than the Russians, we are fundamentally more robust. We have not had autumn yet. We shall have plenty of fine days before winter sets in."

The perception that "we are more robust" and the predictions that "one thing will take the place of another" and "we shall have plenty of fine days" demonstrate the sway of the action syndrome. Napoleon, unlike Caulaincourt, was not free to indulge in doubt. Not long after this conversation, he was forced by the weather and the Russians to begin a disastrous retreat.

The action syndrome enables the actor to believe he will not fail, because he cannot fail. Replying to the doubts of a critic during the Vietnam War, an official offered:

We're just not as pessimistic as you are.

But what if the North Vietnamese match our air escalation with their ground escalation?

We just don't think that's going to happen.

Just suppose it happens, just assume the worst.

We can't assume what we don't believe.

Such an exchange deepens the commitment of the actor. The reply to the threat against the world-model is greater certainty.

Listen to this exchange that Lincoln Steffens, the leading muckraker during the early decades of the 20th century, reported in his autobiography.

> ...[Rudoph Spreckels, a San Francisco financier] was prophesizing one day with such certainty that I halted him to recall that a year before he had made an equally positive prediction, that the Federal Reserve Bank bill, if passed, would precipitate a bank panic.
>
> 'Well what of that?,' he demanded.
>
> 'Nothing, only the bank bill did pass, and there was no bank panic.'
>
> "Well, and what of that?"
>
> "Only this, that if you can be so wrong once you may be wrong again. You should not be so sure of things."
>
> He laid his hand on my arm, and more as a plea than a command, he said, "Don't — don't make me doubt my convictions. I cannot act unless I am sure."
>
> ... Practical men, so called, seem to pass through distinct periods; they consult and think till they decide, and then they will not hear or hesitate any more. They shut their eyes and go, blind

Aided by the action syndrome, the actor evaluating the course followed, after looking back on perception, decision, and action, will see it all in the best light. President Johnson, in retirement, felt his decisions about the Vietnam War had been right:

> The war was horrible, I knew that. We lost 50,000 people. But if I hadn't entered the war, I would have lost World War III, and everything would have been far worse than we could have imagined.

So even the audit, the post-mortem, is warped by the syndrome. One may always argue that, without the action, things would have been much worse.

Nothing is as persuasive as the force of conviction. The person who cannot persuade himself cannot expect to persuade anyone else. Moreover, by persuading another he also persuades himself. In a natural leader, whose very personality connotes power, we can expect to find the most highly developed form of the action syndrome.

In matters of state the syndrome operates now as it did in Xerxes' time. These words of C. P. Snow, once a British government official, catch the mood of the action syndrome:

> We can collect quite a few tips from the Tizard-Lindemann [two leading scientists in Great Britain during World War II] story. For instance, the prime importance, in any crisis of action, of being positive what you want to do and of being able to explain it. It is not so relevant whether you are right or wrong. That is a second-order effect. But it is cardinal that you should be positive.

The scale of our actions, the duration of their impact, and the shrunken margin of error demand actors who stay flexible, who preserve the option to turn back. In this context, the syndrome can do more harm than good. Though we need the flexibility of Artabanus and Caulaincourt, the action syndrome gives us the rigidity of Xerxes and Napoleon.

If the action syndrome cannot be subdued, at least we can compensate for it. Since it thrives in the atmosphere of a great gamble, in particular in the vicinity of a GRIMP, we may prefer enterprises that can be divided into smaller parts to those that demand a single, large commitment. When we see signs of the action syndrome in ourselves or in others, we can at least discount the perceptions, choices, and predictions made under its powerful influence.

30 Limits

Action, through the action syndrome, impacts choice, prediction, and perception. Choice, especially choice between incomparables, limits the accuracy of predictions, colors our perception, and shapes action. Similarly, both prediction and perception impact the concepts at the other corners of the pyramid.

This pyramid sets limits to our ability to control events. Our predictions, no matter how carefully made, have limited reliabil-

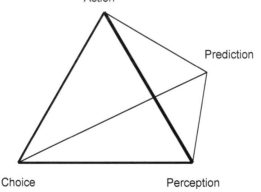

Action

Prediction

Choice   Perception

ity. Our perceptions are subject to distortions originating outside us and within us. Our instinct to model reality, to interpret and absorb it into our world system, is so strong that it is hard to suspend judgment. Once error enters our model, it is not easy to remove it. The act of decision, of choosing, often requires a leap to cross a gap that evades analysis. We make that leap, but we don't know how we do it.

Scholars, who study the four corners of the pyramid, may pin down these limits more accurately than I could in this sketch. Journals with titles such as *Choice, Perception,* and *Forecasting* probe these issues, as do books, such as *Judgment and Decision Making, Judgmental Forecasting,* and *Judgment Under Uncertainty.* However, their research is still in a primitive stage, much as the theory of electricity and magnetism was at the beginning of the 19th century.

Neuroscientists, using magnetic imaging, can peer inside the brain and watch the electrical activity as a person makes a decision. They have already discovered the brain relies on the relative firing rates of synapses and of neurotransmitters, such as dopamine. These rates, influenced by past experience and current stimuli, combine in our brains to allow us to make comparisons and choices.

The neuroscientists have made another discovery, which may be related to the perceptual option and the action syndrome. To introduce their work, I first point out that some customs in our society harm the body. The combination of a sedentary life style at work and at home, together with an abundant supply of cheap high-caloric food has triggered an epidemic of obesity.

Could our customs also harm the mind? Think of the political sound bites that have grown ever shorter, the commercials that flash images at the rate of one every one and a half seconds, the movies that drown the viewer in an uninterrupted blend of crash, fire, and murder. Could these insidiously accustom us to respond instantaneously, simplistically to even the most complex issues? Are we being trained to reply with a gut reaction rather than by a measured analysis, which begins with a calm effort to get the "facts" or at least get as close to the bull's eye as we can?

I raise this only as a question. Perhaps the neuroscientists will be able to answer it. Already they have evidence that one part of the brain responds emotionally and another part analytically.

Advertisers and politicians are watching the research closely, but we should all be interested, as it may shed light on the perceptual option and the action syndrome.

It is time to establish an *Institute of Forecasting*, with the purpose of evaluating forecast accuracy and determining the limits of our ability to predict the future in various areas of human activity. Such an institute, in order to avoid any conflict of interest, would be restricted from making forecasts itself. Its task will not be easy. For instance, how will it judge the accuracy of a forecast? How will it deal with failure to predict an event? This diagram represents the actual future as it unfolds and the future as it had been predicted. The overlap is the correct part of the prediction.

Should it compare the correct predictions, which form the overlap of the two ovals, to the actual future or should the overlap be compared to the total prediction? In the latter case, the prophet

The Predicted Future

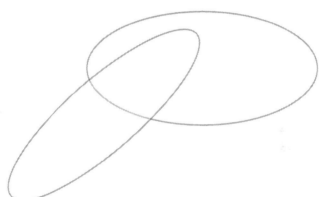

The Actual Future

would not be penalized for the failure to take into consideration major forces.

As I. Gringorten pointed out in "The Verification and Scoring of Weather Forecasts," "a clear distinction should have been made between the utility of a forecast and the skill of the forecaster." That means that the accuracy of a forecast should be judged independently of the many different uses it may have, such as helping a pilot chart a flight plan or a person to decide whether to take an umbrella while shopping.

An *Institute of Choice* and an *Institute of Perception* would have obvious goals and restrictions. Institutes similar to these already exist, such as the *Center for Decision Research* at the University of Chicago. With the aid of experiments, it focuses on how people actually make decisions, rather than depending on a theory of how the imaginary "rational" person should decide.

There is work to be done. As the economist H. Simon wrote in Decision Making and Problem Solving:

> *People cannot usually provide verbal accounts of how they make up their minds, especially when there is uncertainty. The reasons people give for their choices can be shown to be rationalizations not closely related to their real motive. [There are] limits on human rationality. These limits are imposed by the complexity of the world in which we live, the incompleteness and inadequacy of human knowledge, the inconsistencies of individual preference and the inadequacy of the computations we can carry out.*

And there may well be limits on our ability to perceive the future. When I browse through the pages of *The International Journal of Forecasting*, I find reports like these:

> *How well do forecasters predict recessions? The simple answer is: "Not very well." Only two of the sixty recessions that occurred ... were predicted a year in advance ... two-thirds remained undetected by April of the year of the recession.*

And,

> *Our ability to forecast is still so bad that methodologically nobody should throw stones at anyone else and there is room for everybody who has an idea.*

Such lamentations appear after decades of attempts to improve forecasting techniques.

Running through this book is another theme, subliminally, like a subterranean river. This theme, like the action syndrome, ties perception, prediction, and choice together. It is what I will call "belief." I don't mean just religious belief, but belief in its many forms, such as conviction, opinion, attitude, or impression. It's what binds us to a particular model and makes it hard for us to budge from it.

Imagine a person and an assertion. The relation between the two may range anywhere from total endorsement, through indifference, to total rejection. It is hard to be neutral, to stay detached, to resist forming an opinion. In this it resembles our compulsion to model whatever strikes our senses, as illustrated by our responses to the diagram of thirty lines in Chapter 1.

"Belief" implies some degree of attachment to an assertion. It is as though some invisible glue binds us to it. The evidence supporting the belief may be skimpy or plentiful, but the strength of the belief may have no relation to the weight of evidence in its favor or against it. Paradoxically, the weaker the case, the stronger may be the belief. How does a belief form? What sustains it? How is it destroyed? Even though we are mere laypersons, we can look within ourselves and try to answer these questions.

Is there some technique that will help us remain detached, to resist the lure of belief, or at least to delay its onset until we are assured that it is well founded? That takes us back to the chapters called "Veneer" and "The Art of No Opinion."

The least we can do is look within ourselves as we watch our own beliefs form, and persist or dissolve. What we discover will help us withstand the maneuvers of those who try to dangle us on their strings, as well as our own knee-jerk opinions and perceptual options. We can carry out this introspection now, without waiting for the final report of the psychologists.

R. M. Hogarth, in his book *Judgement and Choice,* concluded:

> *Few people seem to be aware that they are continually making all kinds of predictions and evaluative judgements. Indeed, the activity is so common that most of us take it for granted. However, it is precisely those things that we take for granted that should be questioned. It is important to learn the limits of one's judgemental ability.*

I interpret this statement, and the preceding chapters, as warning us not to be too cocky. Our tribe would benefit by cultivating more humility and less certainty.

Commenting on why most economists failed to predict the deepest recession since the Depression, Paul Krugman wrote:

[T]he central cause of the profession's failure was the desire for an all-encompassing, intellectually elegant approach that also gave economists a chance to show off their mathematical prowess ... They turned a blind eye to the limitations of human rationality ... [E]conomists will have to learn how to live with messiness.

We, too, must learn to live with messiness, the unpredictable side effect of our actions, with the irrationality of the way the world and our minds operate.

We should remain aware of our own quirks and limits and, with the aid of the dead-fish principle, protect ourselves from those who would, by exploiting our vulnerabilities, manipulate us. As we reflect on the themes in this book, we should practice resisting the distortions due to the action syndrome. Every day we — both high and low — could repeat several times, "I could be wrong," as a reminder.

On the other hand, we should not abandon our feelings and insights in deference to an expert, whether professional or shaman, who may be more handicapped than we, being in the throes of the action syndrome. We should be especially wary when experts predict, or push a GRIMP, or resort to intimidation by numbers and computers. Our vigilance not only protects ourselves but also helps preserve the essence of our democracy. It may even help rescue the twenty-first century from duplicating the horrors of the twentieth.

31 Be of Good Cheer

After reading the manuscript of this book, a friend, Mary Wind, lamented, "What you say is true and convincing, but it all seems so hopeless. I ended up in a state of despair. You didn't propose a solution."

I was surprised by this reaction, since I have been living for years with the reality I describe without being depressed. Besides, I have included many suggestions of what we can do, without offering some single magic act that at one blow would resolve the problems I mention. Some battles may go on forever. What we can do depends on how much energy, time, or money we have after working at our job and taking care of our family. And remember that we are not alone. Many others think like us. A massive rally can trump any number of dollars.

If you look back at the chapters you will see that they are full of warnings and bits of advice. Running through them is the theme that just as war is too important to be left to the generals, peace is too important to be left to the politicians. We outsiders have an advantage over the people in power. We are free to change our minds. When they change their minds, they are accused of "flip-flopping," a phrase used by politicians since 1890.

The first chapter set the stage for the whole book. It reminded us that the world in our heads is not the same as the real world. Because our own world has such a flimsy foundation we are easy marks for those who want to control what we believe. So we must be on guard, questioning our own assumptions and watching for the tricks of the manipulators.

I am suggesting for us what Scott McClellan, who served almost three years as press secretary in the George W. Bush administration, regularly attending high-level meetings where big decisions were made, has suggested for future presidents. He proposes a "deputy to serve directly under the president" whose task is to make sure the president maintains "a high level of openness" and transcends partisanship. That may never come to pass. However, we can easily implement that suggestion in our own lives by seeking sources of information that challenge our dearest beliefs — whether newspaper, website, book, or people. We can do this without appointing a deputy to remind us to be open,

The image of the bull's eye (chapter 2) and the rings reminds us that by the time a fact reaches us, it has been distorted, either innocently or with intent to deceive, by omission or by commission. As the mayor of Salt Lake City urged, we can spend a little of the time we spend being entertained by athletes, musicians, and TV on trying to reduce the distortion. Is it too much to ask us to read at least one book a year in order to strengthen our role in preserving our democracy? At this moment I am reading the Koran, trying to reach a bull's eye, without relying on others to tell me what it says. We cannot depend on the media to provide the facts and history that would help us make sense of today's headlines.

In the financial collapse of 2008 we don't need to be intimidated by phrases such as "credit default swap." It turns out to be an insurance policy, but its inventor didn't call it a "credit default insurance" because then it would be regulated. As Kevin Phillips in *Bad Money* observes, "Credit derivatives, securitization, and even current account deficits do not lend themselves to conversations in neighborhood bars or beauty parlors. Americans are excusing themselves. Still, if the farmers of more than a century ago could study and understand Sherman Silver Purchase Act provisions and details of the nationwide currency shrinkage — and many studied and somehow managed — can't we expect as much today?" We should, out of sheer self-interest.

By recounting my oscillating response to *The Skeptical Environmentalist* I illustrated (chapter 3) how we can be batted about like a ping-pong ball. That should remind us how vulnerable we are and to avoid having too much faith in our own views or in the pronouncements of our leaders. That led to the conclusion that we should be slow to judge, advice that goes back two millennia. The dead-fish principle (chapter 7) may help control our impulse to jump too quickly to a conclusion.

The choice between incomparables (chapter 8) is important for two reasons. First, it is easily influenced by those who want to persuade us. Second, it adds to the murkiness of the future. Even a choice of the form "to do or not to do" is a choice between incomparables, with each of the options creating a world.

The discussion of prediction (chapters 14, 15) warns us to be on guard about any statement that uses the future tense, whether disguised as a promise or as a fact. Such assertions should be automatically discounted and filed in the "maybe, who knows?" folder in the back of our minds. If the folder is on paper or stored in your computer, you could even check up on them later, but that may only encourage cynicism.

The GRIMP (chapter 17) reminds us that small and gradual may be wiser than gigantic and abrupt. When someone proposes a GRIMP, we should be ready to explore alternatives.

We can keep in mind the two types of experts (chapter 19) and expert-creep (chapter 20). Our experts may not be any wiser than we are, or know more than we do. We should be ready to call their bluff, especially if they use numbers to overwhelm us.

I don't expect the world will insist that predictions be made in numerical form. However, if we grade a prediction by a percentage, then at least we remind everyone, including ourselves, that there is a grey area between the inevitable and the impossible. That might restrain some actors and even avoid some rash acts.

When we face an issue, we can ask, "Is this subject to the scientific method?" (chapter 25) If it is, urge that it be applied. If not, be alert to the presence of shamans and their prophecies.

We can compensate for the power of the action syndrome (chapter 29) by reminding ourselves and our leaders to be less dogmatic and more open to the other side. A little more humility may turn down the rhetoric, whose shrillness is inversely proportional to the solidity of its basis.

In a nutshell, this book argues for more humility in ourselves and in the insiders, and at the same time that the distance separating us from them is smaller than we like to assume.

Underlying the whole book is the theme (chapter 30) that there are limits — limits on our ability to see into the future, limits on the wisdom we can bring to making a choice, limits to our understanding of the present and the past.

The book is about attitude. It is not a manual, like the instructions for assembling a new bookcase. It is, rather, one outsider's attempt to respond to Jefferson's insight that a democracy depends on an informed citizenry.

And we do matter. Letters to Congress are counted. Presidents push their agenda by persuading us to put pressure on Congress. If we tithe our time for democracy, we can make it work, in spite of the efforts of powerful groups working behind the curtain to take it over. Then we can expect our letters, phone calls, and votes to represent our interests, not those of the insiders.

References

1 The Model

5. Jesuit and atheist: personal communication from E. J. Mac-Shane.

6. Roosevelt letter: *The Letters of Theodore Roosevelt*, Cambridge, Harvard University, 1952, Volume 5: 421.

7. Johnson: Robert McNamara, *In Retrospect*, New York, Times Books, 1995: 220.

2. The Bull's Eye and the Rings

11. Friedman: Thomas Friedman, "Cars, Kabul, and Banks," *New York Times*, December 14, 2008.

11. Machiavelli: Nicolo Machiavelli, *The Prince*, New York, Penguin, 1979: 100-101.

11. Gingrich: Connie Bruck, "The Politics of Perception," *New Yorker*, October 9, 1995: 59.

12. Bush: Katherine Q. Seelye, "Kerry Says His Economic Plan Calls for Federal Spending Caps and Clinton-Era Rules," *New York Times*, April 8, 2004.

12. Kuo: David Kuo, *Tempting Faith*, New York, Free Press, 2006: 229.

12, Rendon: Sheldon Hampton and John Stauber, *Weapons of Mass Deception*, New York, Tarcher/Penguin, 2003: 4.

13. facsimile: Elin Schoen Brockman, "For the Jaded Esthete, A Dose of the Very Real," *New York Times*, May 16, 1999.

14. Ellsberg, Daniel Ellsberg,*Secrets*, New York, Viking, 2002: 237.

3. Veneer

16. Bjorn Lomborg: Bjorn Lomborg, *The Skeptical Environmentalist,* Cambridge, United Kingdom, Cambridge University Press, 2001: xxi.

16. Washington Post: "Why All Those Dire Predictions Have No Future," *Washington Post,* October 2, 2001.

17. intentionally selects: Emily Matthews, "Not Seeing the Forest for the Trees," *Grist Magazine,* December 12, 2001 (web).

17. international statistics: Chris Lavers, "You've Never Had It So Good," *The Guardian,* September 1, 2001 (web).

18. scientific dishonesty: Andrew Revkin, "Environment and Science: Danes Rebuke 'Skeptic'," *New York Times,* January 8, 2003.

18. panel had erred: Andrew Revkin, "Danish Ethics Panel Censured for Critique of Book," *New York Times,* December 23, 2003.

18. United Nations: Kimberley A. Strassel, "The Weekend Interview with Bjorn Lomborg," *Wall Street Journal,* July 8-9, 2006.

Further reading: Nicholas Wade, "From an Unlikely Quarter, Eco-Optimism," *New York Times,* August 7, 2001.

19. Kuo: David Kuo, *Tempting Faith,* New York, Free Press, 2006: 226.

4. Distortion by Omission

21. Paul O'Neill: Ron Susskind, *The Price of Loyalty.* New York. Simon and Schuster, 2004: 314.

21. Welfare Queen: Liberalism Resurgent web site, Steve Kangas, 2004.

21. killing ground: Scott McClellan, *What Happened,* New York, Public Affairs, 2008:

22. tobacco: "Tobacco Memo Advised Burying Adverse Study," *New York Times,* September 19, 1996.

23. Humphrey: Michael R. Beschloss, *Taking Charge,* New York, Simon and Schuster, 1997: 499.

24. McClellan: Scott McClellan, *What Happened,* New York, Public Affairs, 2008: 229.

24. Chile: Peter Kornbluh, *The Pinochet Files,* New York, The New Press, 1993: 79.

25. Gagarin: William J. Broad, "Russian Space Mementos Show Gagarin's Ride Was a Rough One," *New York Times*, March 5, 1996.
25. photographs: Philip Knightley, *The First Casualty*, New York, Harcourt Brace Jovanovich., 1975: 99. (JohnsHopkins University Press, 2002)

5. Distortion by Commission

27. Pentagon: Sheldon Rampton and John Stauber, *Weapons of Mass Deception*, New York, Tarcher/Penguin, 2003: 5.
28. mitigate: *War Made Easy*, Norman Solomon, Wiley, New York, 2005: 218.
28. Friday: "Thompson complains about Bush, deficit, *Davis Enterprise*, December 19, 2006.
29. Sol Wachtler: My Life in Prison: The Odyssey of New York's Top Judge, *Sacramento Bee*, March 24, 1996.
30. Lindsey: Scott McLellan, *What Happened*, Public Affairs, New York, 2008: 122-123
30. Cindy Watson, Free Speech for Sale, A Bill Moyers Special, PBS, June 8, 1999.
31. bias: Eric Alterman, *What Liberal Media?*, Basic Books, New York, 1993: 2.
31. Libya: see also Robert Musil and Martin Butcher, "The Real Threat of Nuclear Terror," *New York Times* (letter to editor), March 15, 2004.
33. Names: Jane Fritsch: "Friend or Foe? Nature Groups Say Names Lie," *New York Times*, March 25, 1996.
34. smoking restrictions: Tom Elias, "About Time for Truth in Initiatives," *Davis Enterprise* (syndicated), January 28, 2000. (See also David Hevarg, "The Big Green Spin Machine," *The Amicus Journal, Natural Resources Defense Journal*, Summer, 1996: 13-21).
34. estate tax: Lizette Alvarez, " In 2 Parties' War of Words, Shibboleths Emerge as Clear Winner," *New York Times*, April 27, 2001.
35. Senator Dick: *Congressional Record* – Senate, August 5, 1909: 4958.
35. poll: "It Depends on How You Ask," *New York Times*, January 30, 2000.

6. The Art of No Opinion

37. 9/11: *The 9/11 Commission Report*, New York, W. W. Norton: xvi.

37. CIA: *Imperial Hubris*, Michael Scheuer, Washington, D. C.. Brassey's, Inc.: 8.

38. Stephen Kinzer, *All the Shah's Men*, New York, Wiley, 1993.

38. Jacoby: Jeff Jacoby, "The Cost of a Death-Penalty Moratorium," *The Boston Globe*, June 6, 2002.

39. rate: Uniform Crime Reports of the Federal Bureau of Investigation.

40. Ehrlich: Hugo Bedau, *The Death Penalty in America.*, 3rd Edition, New York, Oxford University Press: 130.

7. The Dead-Fish Principle

45. Lesly: *Lesly's Handbook of Public Opinion and Communication*, Contemporary Books, 1998: 465.

46. playbook: "Why big Jim Always Arrives Late," *Suburban Sun-Times*, December 1, 1978.

47. tax-cut: Paul Krugman, "The Tax-Cut Con," *New York Times Magazine.* September 14, 2003: 54.

CHOICE

8. The Incomparables

51. Lincoln: Doris K. Goodwin, *Team of Rivals*, New York, Simon and Schuster, 2005: 340.

51. Yergin: Daniel Yergin, *The Prize*, New York, Simon and Schuster, 1992: 787.

52. Dubus: Andre Dubs III, *House of Sand and Fog,* New York, W.W.Norton, 1999: 84.

52. Sartre: Jean-Paul Sartre, *Essays in Existentialism*, New York, The Citadel Press, 1968: 42.

52. O'Keefe: Sean O'Keefe, "Advancing Both Science and Safety," *New York Times*, March 13, 2004.

53. McNamara: Robert S. McNamara, *In Retrospect*, New York, Times Books, 1995: 226.

53. NHTSA: Public Law 94-163 December 22, 1975: 905.

55. dam: Frederic D. Schwarz, "Dams in Distress," *Invention and Technology*, Fall, 2002: 10-11.

55. Babbitt: Sam Howe Verhovek, "They Exist. Therefore They Are. But, Do You care?," *New York Times*, October 17, 1999.

55. Federal: Federal Land Policy and Management Act of 1976, Public Law 94-579, October 21, 1976, 90 STAT. 2748.

56. Connaughton: Douglas Jehl "On Environmental Rules, Bush Sees a Balance, Critics a Threat," *New York Times*, February 23, 2003.

57. Pinchot: Harold Wood, "Pinchot and Mather: How the Forest Service and Park Service Got That Way," *Not Man Apart*, December, 1976.

57. Muir: ibid.

57. Hogarth: Robin Hogarth: *Judgement and Choice*: The Psychology of Decision. New York. John Wiley & Sons. 1986: 232.

9. Hidden Choice

59. boxing match: Richard Sandomir, "The $100 Million Fight: Get Set for a Rematch," *New York Times*, November 12, 1996.

60. weight loss: David Wallis, " Starving for Attention," *New York Times*, June 30, 1996.

61. Iraq: John S. Friedman, "The Iraq Index," *The Nation*, December 19, 2005: 23-25.

61. Redwood Park: Dudley McFadden, "Spending priorities," *Davis Enterprise*, May 16, 2001.

62. Eisenhower: Speech to American Society of Newspaper Editors, April 16, 1953.

63. dozens of ways: Dudley McFadden, "Spending Priorities," *Davis Enterprise,* May 16, 2001.

63. Pollitt: Kathy Pollitt, "Who Needs Christmas? They Do!," *The Nation*, December 29, 2003: 9.

64. Jackson: Stanton J. Price, "Protests that Count," *New York Times*, February 1, 2004.

65. Singer: Peter Singer, "The Singer Solution to World Poverty," *New York Times Magazine*, September 5, 1999: 60-63.

65. Singer: Peter Singer, "What Should a Billionaire Give – and What Should You?," *New York Times Magazine*, December 17, 2006: 58-63, 80, 83, 87.

NUMBER

10. Beware the Number

70. Schoenberg: Joan Peyser, *Twentieth Century Music*, New York, Macmillan, 1979: 11.
70. Wilson: Margaret Macmillan, *Paris*, 1919, New York, Random House, 2001: 94.
71. drugs and PFA: Christopher S. Wren, "Phantom Numbers Haunt the War on Drugs," *New York Times*, April 20, 1997.
71. children: Steven A. Holmes, "It's Awful! It's Terrible! It's ... Never Mind," *New York Times.* July 6, 1997.
71. Engineers: Gerald W. Bracey, "Heard the One About the 600,000 Chinese Engineers?," *Washington Post*, May 21, 2006.
73: Morgenstern: Oskar Morgenstern, *On the Accuracy of Economic Observations*, Princeton, Princeton University Press, 1973: 286.
74. pacification: Clyde Pettit, *The Experts*, Secaucus, Lyle Stuart. 1975: 342.

11. Second Warning about Numbers

77. dice: Martin Gardner, *Wheels, Life, and Other Mathematical Amusements.* San Francisco. W. H. Freeman, 1983: 40-42.

See also Graham Loomes, Chris Starmer, and Robert Sugden, " Observing Violations of Transitivity by Experimental Methods," *Econometrica,* 59 (1991): 425-439.

12. Third Warning about Numbers

84. Guilford: quoted in Harry Hopkins, *The Numbers Game*, London, Secker and Warburg, 1973: 245.

13. Where Did that Number Come From

88. handbook: *Business Cycle Indicators Handbook*, The Conference Board, New York, 2001.

93. Klein: "Assessing Business Cycle Indicators," *Business Cycle Indicators* 4 (1999).

93. Morris: F. S. Morris, "The Leading Indicators Revisited," *Business Economics*, September, 1970: 16 (cited in Molefsky)

93. Barry Molefsky, "An Examination of the Index of Leading Economic Indicators," in *Major Studies and Issue Briefs of the Congressional Research Service 1981-1982 Supplement*, Microfilm, University Publications of America, Inc., Frederick, Maryland.

93. Diebold: F. X. Diebold and G. D. Rudebusch, *Business Cycles*, Princeton, Princeton University Press, 1998: 22.

94. extra payments: "Index Overstates Inflation Rate, U.S. Panel Finds," *Los Angeles Times*, December 4, 1996.

14. A Scale for Uncertainty

98. football: David Leonhardt, "In Football, 6 + 2 Often Equals 6," *New York Times*, January 17, 2000.

100. CIA: Peter Kornbluh, *The Pinochet File*, New York, The New Press, 2003: 25.

100. Volcker: Paul Krugman, "The Dishonesty Thing," *New York Times*, September 10, 2004.

100. Chu: Jon Gertner, The Future Is Drying Up, *New York Times Magazine*, October 21, 2007.

100. Kennedy: Theodore Sorensen. *Kennedy*, New York. Harper & Row, 1965: 705.

101. meteorologist: Irving I. Gringorten, "The Verification and Scoring of Weather Forecasts," *Journal of the American Statistical Association*, volume 46, 1951: 279-296.

101. Kent: Jack Davis, "Sherman Kent and the Profession of Intelligence Analysis," Sherman Kent Center, *Occasional Papers*, volume 1, Number 5, November,2002.(https://www.cia.gov/cia/publications/Kent_Papers/Vol1no5.htm)

101. CIA: Key Judgments From a National Intelligence Estimate on Iran's Nuclear Activity, *New York Times*, December 4, 2007.

102. Rubin: Jacob Weisberg, "Keeping the Boom From Busting," *New York Times Magazine*, July 19, 1998.

102. Tversky: Daniel Kahneman, Paul Slovic, and Amos Tversky, *Judgment under Uncertainty: Heuristics and Biases*, New York, Cambridge University Press, 1982. See also: Tversky: *Preference, Belief, and Similarity, Selected Writings of Amos Tversky*, Ed. Eldar Shafir, MIT Press, Cambridge, MA, 2004.

15. It Will Definitely Happen, Perhaps

106. Simpson: R. H. Simpson, "The Specific Meanings of Certain Terms Indicating Differing Degrees of Frequency," *Quarterly Journal of Speech*, 30, 1944: 328-330.
106. Lichtenstein and Newman: S. Lichtenstein and J. R. Newman, "Empirical Scaling of Common Verbal Phrases Associated with Numerical Probabilities," *Psychonomic Science* 9 (1967): 563-564.
107. Beyth-Marom: Ruth Beyth-Marom, "How Probable is Probable? A Numerical translation of Verbal Probability statements," *Journal of Forecasting* 1 (1982): 257-269.

16. Just Try to Measure It

112. *London Airport: Report of the Commission on the Third London Airport*, HMSO, 1971.
113. PBBS: Planning, Programming, Budgeting; Inquiry of the Subcommittee on National Security and International Relations, United States Senate, 1970.
113. Knorr: ibid: 581.
114. Ross: ibid: 397.
114. Schlesinger: ibid: 135.
115. Wildavsky: ibid: 619.
116. Executive Order: Executive Order 12866 Regulatory Planning and Review, *Federal Register:* September 30, 1993 (Volume 58): 51735.

17. The GRIMP

119. Freedman: D.A. Freedman and P.B.Stark, http://www.stat.berkeley.edu/tech-reports/611.pdf.
120. dam: *Report of the United States Department of the Interior and State of Idaho on Failure of Teton Dam*, GPO, 1976. See also:

"6 Dead, 53 Missing in Idaho Flood; Devastation Is Vast," *New York Times*, June 7, 1976.

123. Brodie: Bernard Brodie, *The Atomic Bomb and American Security*, Memorandum 18, New Haven, November 1, 1945.

123. Kissinger: Henry Kissinger, *Nuclear Weapons and Foreign Policy*, New York. Harper. 1957: 156-157.

123. Kahn: Herman Kahn, *On Thermonuclear War*, Princeton. Princeton University Press, 1960: 21.

18. What is a Job?

127. horse racing: Sarah Armquist, "And they're off," *Davis Enterprise*, January 27, 2005.

128. tobacco: Michael Janofsky, "Spinning the Data on Cigarette Taxes," *New York Times*, June 5, 1993.

128. asteroid: David Streitfeld, "Hanging on After the Big Hang-Up," *Los Angeles Times*, August 17, 2003.

130. Rifkin: Jeremy Rifkin, "Civil Society in the Information Age," *The Nation*, February 26, 1996: 12.

131. case for recycling: Californians Against Waste Call to Action, Sacramento, California, 1979.

131. Eugene Meehan, *The Quality of Federal Policy Making; Programmed Failure in Public Housing*, University of Missouri Press, 1979: 17.

131. automobile repair: Ernest Holsendolph, "Faulty Car Repairs Found Widespread," *New York Times*, May 8, 1979.

131. 53 cents: ibid.

131. Consumer Affairs: website of California Bureau of Auto Repairs, California Department of Consumer Affairs, 2003.

132. bond counsel: Robert Lakechman, "How New York Went for Broke," *The Nation*, December 31, 1977: 714-720.

133. lawyer: Ralph Nader and Mark Green, "Don't Pay those High Legal Bills," *New York Times Magazine*, November 20, 1977.

134. business lunch: Restaurant Protest in Defense of Three-martini Lunch, *Davis Enterprise*, January 25, 1978.

134. Pope Paul VI: Colman McCarthy "The Activist Pope – a World Traveler," *San Francisco Chronicle*, August 17, 1978.

134. Sierra Club: N. B. Goldstein and S. H. Sage, "An Environmental Works Program," *The Nation*, February 11, 1978.

EXPERTS

19. The Two Types of Experts

140. Saint Augustine: St. Augustine, *Confessions*, translated by Maria Boulding O.S.B. New York. Vintage Spiritual Classics. 1997: 128.
140. Schwed: Fred Schwed, Jr. *Where Are the Customers' Yachts or A Good Hard Look at Wall Street*, New York, John Wiley and Sons, 1995: 90-91 (first published by Simon and Schuster in 1940).
141. Byrd: Robert C. Byrd, *Losing America*, New York, W. W. Norton, 2004: 72.
142. Galbraith: John Kenneth Galbraith, *The Great Crash, 1929*, Boston, Houghton Mifflin, 1972: 80.

20. Expert-Creep

147. Chaplin: Rick Lyman, "Celebrities Become Pundits At Their Own Risk," *New York Times*, March 2, 2003.

21. How to Tell A Shaman From a Professional.

150. authentically disagree: A. Mazure, The Dynamics of Technical Controversy, Communications Press, Wash. D.C.,1981.
151. Bernanke: Semiannual Report of the Federal Reserve to Congress, February 24, 2009.
152. strong performance: advertisement, *New York Times*, January 27,2004.

22. The Contract Between Shaman and Layman

156. Vance: "Vance Says U.S. Erred in Joining War in Vietnam," *New York Times*, January 12, 1977.
156. Clubb: O. Edmund Clubb, "Trap in Vietnam," *Progressive*, April, 1962: 16-20.
157. President Carter: Press Conference, January 17, 1979.

157. *The Nation*: "He might Have Read *The Nation*," *The Nation*, February 3, 1979: 101.

157. rugs: John Gregorian, " Iran Rug Business in Big Trouble," *Davis Enterprise*. July 31, 1980.

157. Herodotus: *History*, New York, Tudor, 1947: 39.

158. Supreme Court: Linda Greenhouse, "Protecting Its Mystique," *New York Times*, May 27, 1993.

158. Nuclear regulatory: David Burnham, " Excerpts From Nuclear Mishap Talks," *New York Times*, April 14, 1979.

159. magic: Peter Eldin, *The Magic Handbook*, New York, Aladdin, 1985.

160. Galbraith: Deborah Solomon, "The Populist," *New York Times Magazine*, November 2, 2008.

AUDIT AND PROPHECY

23. The Audit

164. former administrator: "A Safe Street Act, But Few Safe Streets," *New York Times*, April 12, 1975.

165. Roy: Arundhati Roy, "Shall We Leave It to the Experts?," *The Nation*. February 18, 2002, 16-20.

165. Megaprojects: B.Flyvbjerg, N. Bruzelius, W. Rothengatter, *Megaprojects and Risk*, Cambridge, Cambridge University Press, 2003: 11.

166. Ellsberg: Daniel Ellsberg, *Secrets*, New York, Viking: 141.

167. Pettit: C. E. Pettit, *The Experts*, Secaucus, Lyle Stuart, Inc., 1975.

167. Morse: ibid.

168. *New York Times*: May 4, 1975

168. *Publishers' Weekly*: September 4, 1974.

168. *Best Sellers*: February 15, 1975.

169. Cerf: C. Cerf and V.Navasky, *The Experts Speak*, New York, Villard, 1998.

24. Spinoff and Side Effect

171. relief can harm: Paul Lewis, "Downside of Doing Good: Disaster Relief Can Harm," *New York Times*, February 27, 1999.
172. Spinoff: *Spinoff 1976 a Bicentennial Report*, NASA.

25. The Scientific Method

177. Los Angeles: Martin Reiser, Louise Ludwig, Susan Saxe, and Claire Wagner, "An Evaluation of the Use of Psychics in the Investigation of Major Crimes," *Journal of Police Science and Administration* 7 (1979): 18-25.
177. Detectives: Nels Klyver and Martin Reiser, "A Comparison of Psychics, Detectives, and Students in the Investigation of Major Crimes," in *Police Psychology*, M. Reiser, Ed, Los Angeles. Lehi Publishing Company: 260-267.
177. similar experiment: Richard Wiseman, Donald West, and Roy Stemman, "An Experimental Test of Psychic Detection," *Journal of the Society for Psychical Research* 61 (1994): 34-45.
179. Tart: Charles Tart, John Palmer, and Dana Redington, "Effects of Immediate Feedback on ESP Performance: A Second Study," *Journal of the American Society for Psychical Research* 73 (1979): 151-165.
180. Coronary care: Randolph Byrd, "Positive Therapeutic Effects of Intercessory Prayer in a Coronary Care Unit Population," *Southern Medical Journal* 61 (1988): 826-829. See also: William Harris et al, "A Randomized, Controlled Trial of the Effects of Remote, Intercessory Prayer on Outcomes in Patients Admitted to the Coronary Care Unit," *Arch. Intern. Med.* 159: 2273-2278.
181. Double-blind study: Herbert Benson et al., "Study of the Therapeutic Effects of Intercessory Prayer (STEP) in Cardiac Bypass Patients," *American Heart Journal*, April, 2006: 934-942.
181. drunk drivers: Sherman Stein, "Risk Factors of Sober and Drunk Drivers by Time of Day," *Alcohol, Drugs, and Driving*, 5 (1989); 215-227.
182. Dowser: J. T. Enright, "Testing Dowsing," *Skeptical Inquirer*, January, 1999: 1-15.
182. Caltrans: Stacey Solie, "Dante Caliv: Water Witch for Hire," *Point Reyes Light*, December 28, 2006.

26. Modeling the Future

187. Goering: Gustav Gilbert, *Nuremberg Diary*, Cambridge, DeCapo Press, 1995 (Farrar Straus, 1947): 278-279.

191. Soros: Judy Woodruff, "The Financial Crisis: An Interview With George Soros," *New York Review of Books*, May 15, 2008.

27. Casual Audits

193. Bloch: Jean de Bloch, "South Africa and Europe," *North American Review*, 174, 1902: 489-504.

(See also Jean de Bloch, *The Future of War*, translated by W. T. Stead, Boston, Ginn, 1899.)

194. Greenspan: Peter S. Goodman, "Taking Hard New Look at a Greespan Legacy," *New York Times*, October 9, 2008.

195. Brill: "Pundit Scorecard," *Brill's*, February, 1999: 29.

197. Boeing: Anthony J. Parisi, "Boeing Earnings Double on 75% Advance in Sales," *New York Times*, May 8, 1979.

297. Bunge: Mario Bunge, "A decision theoretic model of the American war in Vietnam," *Technological Forecasting and Social Change* 3 (1973): 323-338.

199. keeping the same means: S, K. Stein, "Opinion In, Opinion Out," ibid 19 (1981): 7-14.

199. Riegle: *Congressional Record* – Senate, September 24, 1993.

199. Durenberger: ibid.

200. Stiglitz: Joseph Stiglitz," The Broken Promise of NAFTA," *New York Times*, January 6, 2004.

201. Mahmoud: Essam Mahmoud, "Accuracy in Forecasting," *Journal of Forecasting* 3 (1984): 139-160.

201. Makridakis: S. Makridakis and Michele Hibon," The M-3 Competition: Results, Conclusions, and Implications," *International Journal of Forecasting* 16 (2000): 451-476.

201. Wachs: Martin Wachs, "Forecasts in Urban Transportation Planning: Uses, Methods, and Dilemmas," in Kenneth Land and Stephen Schneider. *Forecasting in Social and Natural Sciences.* Boston, D. Reidel, 1987: 61-80.

202. Cayne: David Leonhardt, "Forecast Too Sunny? Try the Anxious Index," *New York Times*, September 1, 2002.

28. Serious Audits or Foresight in Hindsight

206. Cowles: Alfred Cowles 3rd, "Can Stock Market forecasters Forecast?," *Econometrica* 1 (1938): 309-324.

206. Cocozza: Joseph Cocozza and Henry Steadman, "An Example of Misplaced Confidence in Experts," *Social Problems* 25 (1978): 265-275.

207. Tetlock: Philip. E. Tetlock," Close-Call Counterfactuals and Belief-System Defenses: I Was Not Almost Wrong But I Was Almost Right," *Journal of Personality and Social Psychology* 75 (1998): 639-652. (See also Philip E. Tetlock, "Theory-Driven Reasoning about Plausible Pasts and Probable Futures in World Politics: Are We Prisoners of Our Preconceptions?,"*American Journal of Political Science* 43 (1999): 335-366.)

208. Ormerod: Paul Ormerod, *The Death of Economics*, London, Faber and Faber, 1994: 3.

208 Ahlburg: Dennis Ahlburg," How Accurate are the U.S. Bureau of the Census Projections of Total Live Births," *Journal of Forecasting* 1 (1982); 365-374.

209. Jervis: Robert Jervis, "The future of World Politics: Will It Resemble the Past?" *International Security* 16, (1991-1992): 39-73.

CONCLUSION

29. The Action Syndrome

214. Stein: Sherman Stein, *Strength in Numbers*, New York, John Wiley & Sons, 1996.

214. stress syndrome: Hans Selye, *The Stress of Life*, New York, McGraw-Hill, 1956.

216. Artabanus: Herodotus, *History*, New York, Tudor, 1947: 374.

217. Soviet response: Graham T. Allison, *Essence of Decision*. Boston. Little Brown. 1971: 198, 204.

217. Bay of Pigs: Theodore Sorensen, *Kennedy*, New York, Harper and Row, 1965: 309.

218. McKinley: Charles S. Olcott, *The Life of William McKinley*, Boston, Houghton Mifflin, 1916, volume 2: 110-111.

218. Freud: Theodore Reik, *Listening with the Third Ear*, Farrar, Straus, New York, 1948: Introduction.

219. essence of ultimate decision: Graham T. Allison, *Essence of Decision.* Boston, Little Brown, 1971: i

219. lingered in Moscow: General de Caulaincourt, *With Napoleon in Russia.* New York, Morrow, 1935: 154-155.

221. Steffens: Lincoln Steffens, *The Autobiography of Lincoln Steffens*, New York, Harcourt, Brace and Company, 1993: 633.

221. Johnson: Doris Kearns Goodwin, "Back at the LBJ Ranch," *New York Times Magazine*, November 13, 1977; 43.

222. C. P. Snow: C. P. Snow, *Science and Government*, Cambridge, Harvard University Press, 1961: 66.   Further reading: Dorner, Dietrich, *The Logic of Failure*, Reading, Addison-Wesley, 1997. (This is essentially an experimental investigation of the defects of the action syndrome.)

30. Limits

226. Simon: Herbert A. Simon and Associates, "Decision Making and Problem Solving," in *Decisionmaking*, Mary Zey, Ed. Newbury Park, Sage, 1992: 32-53.

226. Still so bad: Philip A. Klein, "Victor Zarnowitz: An Interview," *International Journal of Forecasting* 18 (2002): 131-151.

227. Hogarth: Robin M Hogarth,. *Judgement and Choice*, Second Edition, New York, John Wiley & Sons, 1986: 232.   See also William Goldstein and Robin M. Hogarth. *Research on Judgment and Decision Making*, New York, Cambridge University Press, 1996: 4.

228. Krugman: Paul Krugman, "How do economists get it so wrong?" *New York Times Magazine*, September 6, 2009: 36-43

31. Be of Good Cheer

230. McClellan; Scott McClellan, *What Happened*, Public Affairs, New York, 2008: 316.

230. Phillips: Phillips, Kevin, *Bad Money*, Viking, New York, 2008: 52.

Special Terms

Name Index

Subject Index

ABOUT THE AUTHOR

Sherman Stein is professor emeritus of mathematics at the University of California at Davis. He is the author of *How the Other Half Thinks: Adventures in Mathematical Reasoning* (McGraw-Hill, 2002), *Strength in Numbers: Discovering the Joy and Power of Mathematics in Everyday Life* (Wiley, 1999) and *Mathematics: The Man-Made Universe* (Dover Publications, 1998).

After growing up in Minneapolis and Los Angeles, Stein spent his undergraduate years at Caltech and received his Ph.D. from Columbia University. He lives in Davis, California, where he enjoys, bicycling, walking, painting and keeping tabs on three children and seven grandchildren.

COLOPHON

Peter Renz designed and set this book using the Lucida family of fonts and Adobe InDesign software. The technical drawings were done in Adobe Illustrator and graphs were done using Mathematica™. We thank Wolfram Research Incorporated for the use of its software. The cartoons are by John Johnson.

4612736

Made in the USA
Charleston, SC
19 February 2010